WebRTC Blueprints

Develop your very own media applications
and services using WebRTC

Andrii Sergiienko

BIRMINGHAM - MUMBAI

WebRTC Blueprints

First published: May 2014

Production Reference: 1080514

Published by Packt Publishing Ltd.
Livery Place
35 Livery Street
Birmingham B3 2PB, UK.

ISBN 978-1-78398-310-0

www.packtpub.com

Cover Image by Manu Gangadhar (manug30@gmail.com)

Credits

Author
Andrii Sergiienko

Reviewers
Alessandro Arrichiello
Antón Román Portabales

Commissioning Editor
Usha Iyer

Acquisition Editors
Kevin Colaco
Rubal Kaur

Content Development Editor
Manasi Pandire

Technical Editors
Krishnaveni Haridas
Manal Pednekar

Copy Editors
Dipti Kapadia
Kirti Pai
Stuti Srivastava

Project Coordinator
Sanghamitra Deb

Proofreaders
Stephen Copestake
Maria Gould
Ameesha Green
Paul Hindle

Indexer
Monica Ajmera Mehta

Graphics
Disha Haria
Yuvraj Mannari

Production Coordinators
Nilesh Bambardekar
Arvindkumar Gupta

Cover Work
Nilesh Bambardekar
Arvindkumar Gupta

About the Author

Andrii Sergiienko is a computer software developer from Ukraine, who is passionate about information technologies and traveling. He has lived in different places and seen different kinds of cultures. Over the years, he has lived in Russia, Belarus, Mongolia, Buryatia, and Siberia. He likes to travel across Europe by auto.

From his early childhood, Andrii was interested in computer programming and hardware; he took his first steps in these fields more than 20 years ago. Andrii has experience with a wide set of languages such as C, C++, Java, Assembler, Erlang, JavaScript, and PHP. He has also worked with technologies such as Riak, shell scripting, computer networks, and security.

In his career, Andrii has worked for both small local companies such as domestic ISPs and large world corporations such as Hewlett Packard. He has also started his own companies, some of which were relatively successful; others failed.

Today, Andrii is the founder of Oslikas, a computer software company that has its headquarters in Estonia. The company is focused on modern IT technologies and solutions. They also develop a full-stack framework to create rich media WebRTC applications and services. You can read more about Oslikas at http://www.oslikas.com.

Acknowledgments

Working on this book was a really great and interesting experience for me, full of brainstorming and emotions. All this would definitely be impossible without the help of certain people. This is the time to say thank you.

First of all, I would like to thank my parents, Olga and Alexander, for providing me with a happy childhood that shaped my future and my career.

I would like to thank my wife, Inna, for her patience, encouragement, and support during these tough times and throughout the process of writing this book.

I would also like to thank the entire team at Packt Publishing. These guys are doing really great work and making the world better. While I was in direct contact with some of the people who were working on the book, others stay unknown to me. I know that a lot of people spent a piece of their lives to make this book possible. Thank you all, guys!

About the Reviewers

Alessandro Arrichiello is a computer enthusiast; he graduated in Computer Engineering from the University of Naples Federico II.

He has a passion for and knowledge of GNU/Linux systems, which started at the age of 14 and continues to this day. He is an independent Android developer on Google Play Store and has strong knowledge of C++, Java, and its derivatives. He also has experience with many other kinds of interpreted languages such as Perl, PHP, and Python.

Alessandro is a proud open source supporter, and he has started and contributed to many collaborative projects developed for academic purposes.

Recently, he enriched his knowledge on network monitoring, focusing on penetration testing and network security in general.

At the moment, Alessandro is working as a software engineer in the Communications and Media Solution group of Hewlett Packard in Milan, Italy. He's involved in many business projects as a developer and technology consultant.

I wish to thank my brother, Gianluca, and my parents for their support during all the activities I've done to review this book. I also wish to thank my girlfriend, Tecla, for waiting all the times I was busy testing and reviewing all the chapters of this book.

Antón Román Portabales is the CTO of Quobis. After graduating in Telecommunications Engineering, he began with VoIP, working for Motorola as an IMS developer. In 2008, he left Motorola to join Quobis, a Spanish company focused on SIP interconnection, which works for major operators and companies in Europe and South America. In 2010, he finished a pre-PhD program in Telematics Engineering and was the main author of a paper on the use of IMS networks to transmit real-time data from the electrical grid, which was presented in an IEEE conference in 2011.

He has been actively working on WebRTC since 2012, the year Quobis decided to focus on this technology. He recently got involved in IETF activities along with his other colleagues from Quobis. He also frequently participates in VoIP-related open source events.

www.PacktPub.com

Support files, eBooks, discount offers, and more

You might want to visit www.PacktPub.com for support files and downloads related to your book.

Did you know that Packt offers eBook versions of every book published, with PDF and ePub files available? You can upgrade to the eBook version at www.PacktPub.com and as a print book customer, you are entitled to a discount on the eBook copy. Get in touch with us at service@packtpub.com for more details.

At www.PacktPub.com, you can also read a collection of free technical articles, sign up for a range of free newsletters and receive exclusive discounts and offers on Packt books and eBooks.

http://PacktLib.PacktPub.com

Do you need instant solutions to your IT questions? PacktLib is Packt's online digital book library. Here, you can access, read and search across Packt's entire library of books.

Why subscribe?

- Fully searchable across every book published by Packt
- Copy and paste, print and bookmark content
- On demand and accessible via web browser

Free access for Packt account holders

If you have an account with Packt at www.PacktPub.com, you can use this to access PacktLib today and view nine entirely free books. Simply use your login credentials for immediate access.

Table of Contents

Preface

What made me start writing this book is the enthusiasm regarding WebRTC, an open project for browser-based, real-time communication.

Until now, building a good interactive web service was always a big problem. You had to use different solutions for different web browsers, you had to use third-party software components and install them on a client's PC, you had problems with cross-platform support, and so many other problems.

Now we have WebRTC. Its development is still in progress and not all browsers and platforms fully support it yet, but it works great already. With WebRTC, you can easily build a rich, media-interactive website or service, and most of your potential users will be able to use it today without any additional specific efforts.

This great project enables easy development of rich media web services without the need to download/install any additional software components on a server or on a client's PC.

I use WebRTC daily at my job for real-life projects, and I will share my knowledge and recipes in this book.

What is WebRTC?

Web Real-Time Communication (WebRTC) is a new (still under development) open framework for the Web to enable browser-to-browser applications for audio/video calling, video chats, and peer-to-peer file sharing without any additional third-party software/plugins.

It was open sourced by Google in 2011 and includes the fundamental building components for high-quality communication on the Web. These components, when implemented in a browser, can be accessed through a JavaScript API, enabling developers to build their own rich media web applications. Google, Mozilla, and Opera support WebRTC and are involved in the development process.

The following are the major components of the WebRTC API:

- `getUserMedia`: This component allows a web browser to access the camera and microphone
- `PeerConnection`: This component sets up audio/video calls
- `DataChannels`: This component allows browsers to share data through peer-to-peer connections

The WebRTC technology contains a complete stack for voice communications, which includes all the necessary codecs. In addition, it provides software-based AEC (acoustic echo cancellation), AGC (automatic gain control), and noise reduction/suppression.

WebRTC also provides the following modern and powerful possibilities to utilize video communications:

- The VP8 codec
- Conceal packet loss
- Clean up noisy images
- Capture and playback capabilities

Peer-to-peer connections can be established using the built-in key NAT/firewall traversal technology using ICE/STUN/TURN and support proxies. So, you don't need to use any special third-party technologies to build a peer-to-peer communication between the customers located behind a firewall or NAT.

To help mitigate the effects of packet loss and unreliable networks, WebRTC supports dynamic jitter buffers and error concealment techniques for audio or video communications.

Supported platforms and devices

WebRTC is a very new technology and is still being developed. Thus, right now, there are still platforms and web browsers that don't support it at all yet or support partially.

WebRTC is supported in the following desktop browsers:

- Google Chrome Version 23 and higher
- Mozilla Firefox Version 22 and higher
- Opera Version 18 and higher
- Internet Explorer doesn't support WebRTC yet, but this can be solved using the Chrome Component for IE

At the time of writing this book, the web browser WebRTC API is natively supported only in the Android platform.

- Google Chrome Version 29 and higher
- Mozilla Firefox Version 24 and higher
- Opera Mobile Version 12 and higher
- Google Chrome OS

Codecs that are supported in WebRTC

For audio calls, the supported codecs are Opus, G.711, G.722, iLBC, and iSAC.

For video communication, VP8 is the only supported codec at the moment.

Considering that WebRTC is still under development, the list of supported codecs may change in the future.

Why should I use WebRTC?

Currently, there are no easy-to-use, high quality, and complete solutions available that would enable communication using just a web browser. Until today, if you wanted to build a rich media cross-platform web application, you had to use Flash, Java Applets, and a bunch of third-party plugins to make it work. Such solutions usually are heavyweight and difficult to implement and support.

This leads to a situation where we have Internet access in almost every apartment across the world, but we still don't have a simple and effective solution for audio/video rich media applications.

WebRTC is a technology that is intended to solve this situation. It is already integrated with the best voice and video engines that have been deployed on millions of end points over recent years.

With this technology, you can use a universal API and a set of built-in technologies and components to build your applications, and you don't need to keep in mind a bunch of platforms and operating systems you would like your application to support.

Applications you can easily build using WebRTC

The following are the applications you can easily build using WebRTC:

- Peer-to-peer audio/video conferences
- Pre-recorded video streaming
- Desktop screen casting
- Peer-to-peer file sharing and transferring

More ideas

- An interactive language school
- Webinars
- A job interview service
- A distributed radio broadcasting service
- A distance learning school
- An interactive dating service

Again, you don't need to use any additional software or libraries. You have to use just the WebRTC API supported by most web browsers today. It works great for Windows, Linux, or Mac OS X without special efforts from the developer.

I believe that after reading this book, you'll want to build your next interactive media web application using WebRTC.

Benefits of using WebRTC in your business

The following are the benefits of using WebRTC in your business:

- **Reducing costs**: WebRTC is a free and open source technology. You don't need to pay for complex proprietary solutions. IT deployment and support costs can be lowered because now you don't need to deploy special client software for your customers.

- **Plugins**: You don't need plugins at all. Previously, you had to use Flash, Java Applets, and other tricky solutions to build interactive rich media web applications. Customers had to download and install third-party plugins to be able to use your media content. You also had to keep in mind different solutions/plugins for a variety of operating systems and platforms. Now you no longer need to care about this.

- **Peer-to-peer communication**: In most cases, communication will be established directly between your customers and you don't need to have a middle point of contact.

- **Easy to use**: You don't need to be a professional programmer or have a team of certified developers with some kind of specific knowledge. In a basic case, you can easily integrate the WebRTC functionality into your web services/sites by using the JavaScript API or even by using a ready-to-go framework.

- **A single solution for all platforms**: You don't need to develop a special native version of your web service for different platforms (iOS, Android, Windows, and others). WebRTC is developed to be a cross-platform and universal tool.

- **WebRTC is open source and free**: A community can discover new bugs and solve them effectively and quickly. Moreover, it is developed and standardized by the world software companies such as Mozilla, Google, and Opera.

What this book covers

Chapter 1, Developing a WebRTC Application, covers the basics of the technology and building a completed audio/video conference real-life web application. We will also learn about SDP (Session Description Protocol), signaling, client-server sides' interoperation, and configuring the STUN and TURN servers.

Chapter 2, Using the WebRTC Data API, explains how to build a peer-to-peer, cross-platform file sharing web service using the WebRTC Data API.

Chapter 3, The Media Streaming and Screen Casting Services, introduces you to streaming prerecorded, peer-to-peer media content and desktop sharing. In this chapter, you will build a simple application that provides such functionality.

Chapter 4, Security and Authentication, covers security questions and why you shouldn't forget them while developing your applications. So, in this chapter, you will learn how to make your WebRTC solutions secure, why authentication may be very important, and how you can implement this functionality in your products.

Chapter 5, Mobile Platforms, covers how to make your interactive application work great on mobile devices. You will learn about the aspects that will help you develop great WebRTC products keeping mobile devices in mind.

What you need for this book

You don't need any special software to read this book and to make applications. We will use JavaScript for the client side, so you will need a web browser (Chrome is preferable). We will use Erlang for server-side code, so you need an OS compatible with Erlang; for example, you can use MS Windows, but any Linux distribution or Mac OS X would be preferable.

Who this book is for

This book will introduce you to creating interactive media web applications and services using WebRTC. In this book, we will create several web-based applications using WebRTC, including ones for the client side and the server side.

Client-side code will be presented in JavaScript. This is an optimal and simple way to utilize a browser WebRTC API.

Server-side code for applications in the book is written in Erlang. Why Erlang? It is a small language, good for quick prototyping and writing production code in an elegant and powerful way.

Thus, you don't have to be a professional software developer, but you are expected to have programming knowledge in Java, JavaScript, Ruby, Python or other mainstream languages, or at least have typical web development skills.

Conventions

In this book, you will find a number of styles of text that distinguish between different kinds of information. Here are some examples of these styles, and an explanation of their meaning.

Code words in text, database table names, folder names, filenames, file extensions, pathnames, dummy URLs, user input, and Twitter handles are shown as follows: "We can declare our module through the use of the `module` directive."

A block of code is set as follows:

```
{ok, Port} = application:get_env(port),
{ok, Timeout} = application:get_env(timeout),
{ok, Workers} = application:get_env(workers),
```

When we wish to draw your attention to a particular part of a code block, the relevant lines or items are set in bold:

```
{ok, Port} = application:get_env(port),
{ok, Timeout} = application:get_env(timeout),
{ok, Workers} = application:get_env(workers),
```

Any command-line input or output is written as follows:

```
# ln -s /usr/local/www/index.html /usr/local/www/default.html
```

New terms and **important words** are shown in bold. Words that you see on the screen, in menus or dialog boxes for example, appear in the text like this: "Now, you can right-click on the link and select the **Download to...** option."

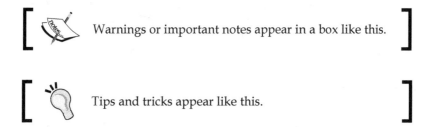

> Warnings or important notes appear in a box like this.

> Tips and tricks appear like this.

Reader feedback

Feedback from our readers is always welcome. Let us know what you think about this book—what you liked or may have disliked. Reader feedback is important for us to develop titles that you really get the most out of.

To send us general feedback, simply send an e-mail to feedback@packtpub.com, and mention the book title via the subject of your message.

If there is a topic that you have expertise in and you are interested in either writing or contributing to a book, see our author guide on www.packtpub.com/authors.

Customer support

Now that you are the proud owner of a Packt book, we have a number of things to help you to get the most from your purchase.

Downloading the example code

You can download the example code files for all Packt books you have purchased from your account at http://www.packtpub.com. If you purchased this book elsewhere, you can visit http://www.packtpub.com/support and register to have the files e-mailed directly to you.

Errata

Although we have taken every care to ensure the accuracy of our content, mistakes do happen. If you find a mistake in one of our books—maybe a mistake in the text or the code—we would be grateful if you would report this to us. By doing so, you can save other readers from frustration and help us improve subsequent versions of this book. If you find any errata, please report them by visiting http://www.packtpub.com/submit-errata, selecting your book, clicking on the **errata submission form** link, and entering the details of your errata. Once your errata are verified, your submission will be accepted and the errata will be uploaded on our website, or added to any list of existing errata, under the Errata section of that title. Any existing errata can be viewed by selecting your title from http://www.packtpub.com/support.

Piracy

Piracy of copyright material on the Internet is an ongoing problem across all media. At Packt, we take the protection of our copyright and licenses very seriously. If you come across any illegal copies of our works, in any form, on the Internet, please provide us with the location address or website name immediately so that we can pursue a remedy.

Please contact us at copyright@packtpub.com with a link to the suspected pirated material.

We appreciate your help in protecting our authors, and our ability to bring you valuable content.

Questions

You can contact us at questions@packtpub.com if you are having a problem with any aspect of the book, and we will do our best to address it.

1
Developing a WebRTC Application

This chapter describes the basics of developing WebRTC media web applications. You will learn how to build a simple peer-to-peer video conference with a web chat that will work through NAT and firewalls (in most cases).

The video conference developed in this chapter consists of two applications: the client-side application and the server-side application.

The client code is written in JavaScript and will be executed in the customer's web browser. This application uses the WebRTC API, handles all the media features, and provides a web page.

The server code will be executed on a server (it can even be your work machine). We need the server application to make our conference work well with peers behind NAT (peers who use private IP addresses). The server code is written in Erlang, and you will also get a brief introduction to this language.

As a bonus, you will get basic knowledge of **Session Traversal Utilities for NAT (STUN)** and **Traversal Using Relay NAT (TURN)** servers. We will discuss them in a more detailed way in *Chapter 4, Security and Authentication*.

Establishing a peer-to-peer connection

WebRTC can't create direct connections between peers without the help of a signaling server. The signaling server is not something standardized that your application can use. Actually, any communication mechanism that allows us to exchange **Session Description Protocol (SDP)** data between peers can be used for signalization. SDP is described in the next section.

A connection between peers and a signaling server is usually called a *signaling channel*. In this chapter, we will use WebSockets to build our signaling server.

Also, peers that exchange SDP data should exchange data about the network connection (even called ICE candidates).

The Session Description Protocol

SDP is an important part of the WebRTC stack. It is used to negotiate on-session/media options while establishing a peer connection.

It is a protocol that is intended to describe multimedia communication sessions for the purposes of session announcement, session invitation, and parameter negotiation. It does not deliver the media data itself, but is used for negotiation between peers of various media types, formats, and all associated properties/options, such as resolution, encryption, and codecs. The set of properties and parameters is usually called a session profile.

Peers have to exchange SDP data using the signaling channel before they can establish a direct connection.

The following is an example of an SDP offer:

```
v=0
o=alice 2890844526 2890844526 IN IP4host.atlanta.example.com
s=
c=IN IP4host.atlanta.example.com
t=0 0
m=audio 49170 RTP/AVP 0 8 97
a=rtpmap:0PCMU/8000
a=rtpmap:8PCMA/8000
a=rtpmap:97iLBC/8000
m=video 51372 RTP/AVP 31 32
a=rtpmap:31H261/90000
a=rtpmap:32MPV/90000
```

Here, we can see that this is a video and audio session, and multiple codecs are offered.

The following is an example of an SDP answer:

```
v=0
o=bob 2808844564 2808844564 IN IP4host.biloxi.example.com
s=
c=IN IP4host.biloxi.example.com
t=0 0
```

```
m=audio 49174 RTP/AVP 0
a=rtpmap:0PCMU/8000
m=video 49170 RTP/AVP 32
a=rtpmap:32MPV/90000
```

Here, we can see that only one codec is accepted in response to the preceding offer.

You can find more SDP sessions' examples at `https://www.rfc-editor.org/rfc/rfc4317.txt`.

You can also find deep details on SDP in the appropriate RFC at `http://tools.ietf.org/html/rfc4566`.

ICE and ICE candidates

Interactive Connectivity Establishment (ICE) is a mechanism that allows peers to establish a connection. In real life, customers usually don't have a direct connection to the Internet; they are connected via network devices/routers, have private IP addresses, use NAT, use network firewalls, and so on. Usually, customers' devices don't have public IP addresses. ICE uses STUN/TURN protocols to make peers establish a connection.

You can find details on ICE in the appropriate RFC at `https://tools.ietf.org/html/rfc5245`.

NAT traversal

WebRTC has an in-built mechanism to use NAT traversal options such as STUN and TURN servers.

In this chapter, we will use public STUN servers, but in real life, you should install and configure your own STUN or TURN server. We will learn how to install a STUN server at the end of this chapter as a bonus to the developed application. We will get into installing and configuring the TURN server in *Chapter 4, Security and Authentication*, while diving into the details.

In most cases, you will use a STUN server; it helps perform a NAT/firewall traversal and establish a direct connection between the peers. In other words, the STUN server is utilized only during the stage of establishing a connection. After the connection has been established, peers will transfer the media data directly between them.

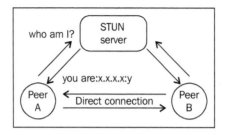

In some cases (unfortunately, they are not so rare), the STUN server won't help you get through a firewall or NAT, and establishing a direct connection between the peers will be impossible, for example, if both peers are behind a symmetric NAT. In this case, the TURN server can help you.

A TURN server works as a retransmitter between the peers. Using the TURN server, all the media data between the peers will be transmitted through the TURN server.

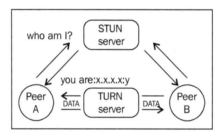

If your application gives a list of several STUN/TURN servers to a WebRTC API, then the web browser will try to use STUN servers first; in case the connection failed, it will try to use the TURN servers automatically.

WebSocket

WebSocket is a protocol that provides full-duplex communication channels over a single TCP connection. This is a relatively young protocol but today all major web browsers, including Chrome, Internet Explorer, Opera, Firefox, and Safari, support it. WebSocket is a replacement for long polling to get a two-way communication between the browser and server.

In this chapter, we will use WebSocket as a transport channel to develop a signaling server for our video conference service. Our peers will communicate with the signaling server using this.

Two important benefits of WebSocket are that it does support HTTPS (secure channel), and it can be used via web proxy (nevertheless, some proxies can block the WebSocket protocol).

Preparing the environment

Let's start with the setup:

1. Create a folder for the whole application somewhere on your disk. Let's call it `my_rtc_project`.
2. Create a directory named `my_rtc_project/www`. Here, we will put all the client-side code (JavaScript files or HTML pages).
3. The signaling server's code will be placed under its separate folder, so create a directory for it and name it `my_rtc_project /apps/rtcserver/src`.
4. Please note that we will use Git, a free and open source-distributed version control system. For Linux boxes, it can be installed using the default package manager. For a Windows system, I recommend that you install and use the implementation available at `https://github.com/msysgit/msysgit`.
5. If you're using a Windows box, install msysgit and add a path to its `bin` folder to your `PATH` environment variable.

Installing Erlang

The signaling server is developed in the Erlang language. Erlang is a great choice to develop server-side applications due to the following reasons:

- It is very comfortable and easy for prototyping
- Its processes (aktors) are very lightweight and cheap
- It does support network operations with no need of any external libraries
- The code has been compiled to a bytecode that runs on a very powerful Erlang Virtual Machine

The following are some great projects developed using Erlang:

- Yaws and Cowboy: These are web servers
- Riak and CouchDB: These are distributed databases

- Cloudant: This is a database service based on the forking of CouchDB
- Ejabberd: This is an XMPP instant messaging service
- Zotonic: This is a content management system
- RabbitMQ: This is a message bus
- Wings 3D: This is a 3D modeler
- GitHub: This is a web-based hosting service for software development projects that use the Git versioning system
- WhatsApp: This is a famous mobile messenger, sold to Facebook
- Call of Duty: This is a computer game that uses Erlang on the server side
- Goldman Sachs: This is a company that uses high-frequency trading computer programs

The following is a very brief history of Erlang:

- **1982–1985**: Ericsson starts experimenting with the programming of telecom, because existing languages weren't suitable for the task.
- **1985–1986**: Ericsson decides it must develop its own language with the desirable features of Lisp, Prolog, and Parlog. The language should have built-in concurrency and error recovery.
- **1987**: First experiments with a new language, Erlang.
- **1988**: Erlang is first used by external users out of the lab.
- **1989**: Ericsson works on the fast implementation of Erlang.
- **1990**: Erlang is presented at ISS'90 and gets new users.
- **1991**: A fast implementation of Erlang is released to users. Erlang is presented at Telecom'91 and gets a compiler and graphic interface.
- **1992**: Erlang gets a lot of new users. Ericsson ports Erlang to new platforms including VxWorks and Macintosh.
- **1993**: Erlang gets distribution. This makes it possible to run homogeneous Erlang systems on heterogeneous hardware. Ericsson starts selling Erlang implementations and Erlang Tools. A separate organization in Ericsson provides support.

Erlang is supported by many platforms. You can download it from the main website, http://www.erlang.org, and install it.

Installing Rebar

Actually, you can write Erlang programs and compile them without using any additional tools. Nevertheless, it is pretty easy to compile Erlang programs using the Rebar tool.

It works like a Make or auto tools for C or C++ applications and makes a developer's life easier.

You can download the Rebar tool from GitHub at `https://github.com/basho/rebar`.

The installation process is pretty simple:

```
git clone git://github.com/rebar/rebar.git
$ cd rebar
$ ./bootstrap

...

==> rebar (compile)
Congratulations!...
```

Now you have the Rebar executable in the folder where you downloaded the Rebar tool. Put it under a folder that is accessible with the PATH environment variable.

Configuring a web server

Configure the web server for your application's domain and point it to the `my_rtc_project/www` folder.

The basic application that we're considering in this chapter works fine without a web server; you can just open the index page in your web browser locally. Nevertheless, in the following chapters, we will touch on more advanced topics that will need to be configured on the web server in order to gain a better understanding of them.

A simple p2p video conference – the browser application

For client-side code that runs in the user's web browser, we will use plain JavaScript.

The WebRTC API functions have different names in different web browsers. To make your application work well with all the browsers, you need to detect which web browser your application is running under and use the appropriate API function names. First of all, we need to implement a helper or an adapter to the WebRTC API functions.

Please note that this situation with different function names is temporary, and after WebRTC is standardized, every browser will support the standard WebRTC API function names. Thus, the WebRTC adapter that we're developing here will probably not be necessary in the future.

Developing a WebRTC API adapter

Create the www/myrtcadapter.js file:

```
function initWebRTCAdapter() {
```

Check whether we're running the file in Firefox:

```
    if (navigator.mozGetUserMedia) {
        webrtcDetectedBrowser = "firefox";
```

Redefine the RTCPeerConnection API function, an entity to keep and control a peer connection itself:

```
RTCPeerConnection = mozRTCPeerConnection;
```

To control the session description entity, we will use RTCSessionDescription:

```
RTCSessionDescription = mozRTCSessionDescription;
```

To support the NAT traversal functionality, we need to use the RTCIceCandidate entity:

```
RTCIceCandidate = mozRTCIceCandidate;
```

We want to get access to audio and video and for that, we need to use the getUserMedia API function:

```
getUserMedia = navigator.mozGetUserMedia.bind(navigator);
```

Besides the WebRTC API functions, different web browsers have different ways to control HTML entities that we need to use. For example, Chrome and Firefox attach the media stream to a media entity (the HTML tag video) in different ways. Thus, we need to redefine additional functions here.

We define the following two functions to attach and reattach the media stream to a video HTML tag:

```
attachMediaStream =
    function(element, stream) {
        element.mozSrcObject = stream;
```

```
        element.play();
    };

reattachMediaStream =
    function(to, from) {
        to.mozSrcObject = from.mozSrcObject;
        to.play();
    };
```

Here, we define two functions to be able to get audio-video tracks from a media stream. Unfortunately, there is no way to do this on a Firefox version that is older than Version 27; thus, here, we just have redundant functions to make our adapter universal:

```
if (!MediaStream.prototype.getVideoTracks) {
        MediaStream.prototype.getVideoTracks =
            function() {
                return [];
            }; };
if (!MediaStream.prototype.getAudioTracks) {
        MediaStream.prototype.getAudioTracks =
            function() {
                return [];
            }; };
        return true;
```

Next, we do the same for Chrome:

```
    } else if (navigator.webkitGetUserMedia) {
webrtcDetectedBrowser = "chrome";

RTCPeerConnection = webkitRTCPeerConnection;
getUserMedia = navigator.webkitGetUserMedia.bind(navigator);
```

As you can see here, we use different ways to support the "attach media stream" functionality for Chrome from the ways we used for Firefox previously:

```
attachMediaStream =
            function(element, stream) {
                element.src = webkitURL.createObjectURL(stream);
            };

reattachMediaStream =
            function(to, from) {
                to.src = from.src;
            };
```

Chrome does support the functionality to get video and audio tracks and so, here, we have a different approach as compared to the one we used for Firefox previously:

```
if (!webkitMediaStream.prototype.getVideoTracks) {
    webkitMediaStream.prototype.getVideoTracks =
        function() {
            return this.videoTracks;
        };
    webkitMediaStream.prototype.getAudioTracks =
        function() {
            return this.audioTracks;
        };
}

if (!webkitRTCPeerConnection.prototype.getLocalStreams) {
    webkitRTCPeerConnection.prototype.getLocalStreams =
        function() {
            return this.localStreams;
        };
    webkitRTCPeerConnection.prototype.getRemoteStreams =
        function() {
            return this.remoteStreams;
        };
}
    return true;
} else return false;
};
```

Developing a WebRTC API wrapper

It is useful to develop a little WebRTC API wrapper library to use it in your application.

Create a file and name it www/myrtclib.js.

First of all, we need to define several variables to control WebRTC entities and use the API. We make them equal to null. However, using our adapter that we developed previously, these variables will refer to appropriate API functions:

```
var RTCPeerConnection = null;
var getUserMedia = null;
var attachMediaStream = null;
var reattachMediaStream = null;
var webrtcDetectedBrowser = null;
```

Here, we keep the virtual room number:

```
var room = null;
```

The `initiator` variable keeps the initiator state that tells us whether we are calling our peer or are waiting for a call:

```
var initiator;
```

The following two variables keep the references to local and remote media streams:

```
var localStream;
var remoteStream;
```

We need the `pc` variable to control a peer connection:

```
var pc = null;
```

As we discussed previously, we need a signaling mechanism to make our connection work. The following variable will store the URL that will point to our signaling server:

```
var signalingURL;
```

The following variables keep the HTML video entities: local and remote. They are just IDs of `video` HTML tags:

```
var localVideo;
var remoteVideo;
```

We want to know whether our signaling channel is ready for operation, and we need a variable to control it:

```
var channelReady;
var channel;
```

Here, we define two STUN servers to support the NAT traversal functionality:

```
var pc_config = {"iceServers":
      [{url:'stun:23.21.150.121'},
       {url:'stun:stun.1.google.com:19302'}]};
```

We also need to define constraints. Using this, we tell a web browser whether we want to use just audio for our conference, or video, or both:

```
var sdpConstraints = {'mandatory': {'OfferToReceiveAudio':true,
'OfferToReceiveVideo':true }};
```

Next, we define several wrapping/helping functions to make our code more universal and reusable.

This is our initialization function. It gets a signaling server's URL and references to local and remote video HTML entities.

Here, we perform the initialization of our API adapter that we developed earlier; after this, we will have universal API function names that we can use under any web browser that supports WebRTC.

After the adapter is initialized, we call the openChannel function that we use to initiate a connection to our signaling server:

```
function myrtclibinit(sURL, lv, rv) {
    signalingURL = sURL;
    localVideo = lv;
    remoteVideo = rv;
    initWebRTCAdapter();
    openChannel();
};
```

The openChannel function opens a connection to our signaling server. Here, we use WebSockets as a transport layer, but it is not mandatory. You can create your own implementation using Ajax, for example, or any other suitable technology that you like the most:

```
function openChannel() {
    channelReady = false;
    channel = new WebSocket(signalingURL);
```

This callback function will be called if our signaling connection has been established successfully. We can't continue if the signaling channel has not been opened:

```
channel.onopen = onChannelOpened;
```

When our peer sends a message during the process of establishing the peer connection, the onChannelMessage callback function will be called and we will be able to react on it:

```
channel.onmessage = onChannelMessage;
```

If the signaling channel has been closed due to some reason (our peer closed its browser or the signaling sever has been powered down), we will get a notification from the onChannelClosed function and react on these two event: show a message to the user or try to re-establish a connection:

```
channel.onclose = onChannelClosed;
};
```

We will get here after the signaling channel has been opened successfully and we can continue and start our conference:

```
function onChannelOpened() {
```

First of all, we need to indicate that the signaling channel is opened and alive:

```
channelReady = true;
```

Here, we try to understand whether we're calling to our peer or we're waiting for a call from it.

We take the URL of our location and try to find the `room` word inside of it. If there is no such word, then we're going to create a virtual room and act passively, waiting for a call from someone.

If we find the `room` word, it means that someone has already created a virtual room and we want to enter it; we're in a calling state and should behave actively, trying to initiate a connection to our peer in the room.

We use the `sendMessage` function to send messages to our signaling server. If the virtual room has not been created yet, then the signaling server will create it and return its room number back to us. In case we have a virtual room number, we ask the signaling server to enter us in to the room; it will parse our message and send it to our peer to initiate the establishment of a direct connection:

```
if(location.search.substring(1,5) == "room") {
  room = location.search.substring(6);
  sendMessage({"type" : "ENTERROOM", "value" : room * 1});
  initiator = true;
} else {
  sendMessage({"type" : "GETROOM", "value" : ""});
  initiator = false;
}
```

We solved our questions with the virtual room; now, we need to ask the browser to give us access to the browser's media resources, video (web camera), and audio (mic):

```
  doGetUserMedia();
};
```

The following function is called when we get a message from our signaling server. Here, we can add some logging or any additional logic but for now, we just need to process the message and react on it:

```
function onChannelMessage(message) {
    processSignalingMessage(message.data);
};
```

The `onChannelClosed` function will be called when the signaling server becomes unavailable (a dropped connection) or if the remote peer has closed the connection (the remote customer has closed its web browser, for example).

In this function, you can also show an appropriate message to your customer or implement any other additional logic.

In the following function, we just indicate that the channel has been closed, and we don't want to transfer any messages to our signaling server:

```
function onChannelClosed() {
    channelReady = false;
};
```

To communicate with the signaling server, we use the `sendMessage` function. It gets a message as a JSON object, makes a string from it, and just transfers it to the signaling server.

When debugging, it is usually helpful to add some kind of message-logging functionality here:

```
function sendMessage(message) {
    var msgString = JSON.stringify(message);
    channel.send(msgString);
};
```

We need to parse messages from the signaling server and react on them, respectively:

```
function processSignalingMessage(message) {
    var msg = JSON.parse(message);
```

If we get an `offer` message, then it means that someone is calling us and we need to answer the call:

```
if (msg.type === 'offer') {
    pc.setRemoteDescription(new RTCSessionDescription(msg));
doAnswer();
```

If we get an `answer` message from the signaling server, it means that we just tried to call someone and it replied with the `answer` message, confirming that it is ready to establish a direct connection:

```
} else if (msg.type === 'answer') {
    pc.setRemoteDescription(new RTCSessionDescription(msg));
```

When a remote peer sends a list of candidates to communicate with, we get this type of message from the signaling server. After we get this message, we add candidates to the peer connection:

```
} else if (msg.type === 'candidate') {
   var candidate = new RTCIceCandidate({sdpMLineIndex:msg.label,
candidate:msg.candidate});
   pc.addIceCandidate(candidate);
```

If we asked the signaling server to create a virtual room, it will send a GETROOM message with the created room's number. We need to store the number to use it later:

```
} else if (msg.type === 'GETROOM') {
   room = msg.value;
```

The OnRoomReceived function is called to implement an additional functionality. Here, we can perform some UI-related actions, such as showing the room's URL to the customers so that they can share it with their friends:

```
OnRoomReceived(room);
```

If we get an URL from our friend that asks us to enter a virtual room but the room number is wrong or outdated, we will get the WRONGROOM message from the signaling server. If so, we are just moving to the index page:

```
} else if (msg.type === 'WRONGROOM') {
   window.location.href = "/";
}
};
```

Here, we're asking the web browser to get us access to the microphone and web camera.

Chrome will show a pop-up window to the user that will ask the user whether he/she wants to provide access or not. So, you will not get access until the user decides. Chrome will ask this every time the user opens your application page. To avoid this and make Chrome remember your choice, you should use the HTTPS connection with the SSL/TLS certificate properly configured in the web server that you're using. Please note that the certificate either needs to be signed by a public CA (Certificate Authority), or by a private CA whose identity has been configured in the browser/client computer. If the browser doesn't trust the certificate automatically and prompts the user to indicate an exception, then your choice will not be remembered by Chrome.

Firefox won't remember the choice, but this behavior can be changed in future:

```
function doGetUserMedia() {
  var constraints = {"audio": true, "video": {"mandatory": {},
"optional": []}};
  try {
```

We ask the WebRTC API to call our callback function, `onUserMediaSuccess`, if we have got the access rights from the user:

```
getUserMedia(constraints, onUserMediaSuccess, null);
```

If we didn't get the access rights, we'll get an exception. Here, you probably want to add some logging and UI logic to inform your customer that something is wrong and we can't continue:

```
    } catch (e) {
  }
};
```

We will get trapped here if we get the access rights to reach the web camera and microphone via the web browser:

```
function onUserMediaSuccess(stream) {
```

We get a video stream from a local web camera and we want to show it on the page, so we're attaching the stream to the `video` tag:

```
attachMediaStream(localVideo, stream);
```

Store the stream in a variable because we want to refer to it later:

```
localStream = stream;
```

Now we're ready to create a direct connection to our peer:

```
createPeerConnection();
```

After the peer connection is created, we put our local video stream into it to make the remote peer see us:

```
pc.addStream(localStream);
```

Check whether we're waiting for a call or we're the caller. If we're the initiator, we call the `doCall` function to initiate an establishment to a direct connection:

```
    if (initiator) doCall();
};
```

The following function will try to create a peer connection—a direct connection between peers:

```
function createPeerConnection() {
```

To improve the security of the connection, we ask the browser to switch on the DTLS-SRTP option. It enables the exchange of the cryptographic parameters and derives the keying material. The key exchange takes place in the media plane and is multiplexed on the same ports as the media itself.

This option was disabled in Chrome by default, but it has been enabled from Version 31 onwards. Nevertheless, we don't want to check the version of a browser used by our customer, so we can't rely on the default settings of the browser:

```
var pc_constraints = {"optional": [{"DtlsSrtpKeyAgreement": true}]};
try {
```

Create a peer connection using the WebRTC API function call. We pass a predefined list of STUN servers and connection configurations to the function:

```
pc = new RTCPeerConnection(pc_config, pc_constraints);
```

Here, we define a callback function to be called when we have to send the ICE candidates to the remote part:

```
pc.onicecandidate = onIceCandidate;
```

When the connection is established, the remote side will add its media stream to the connection. Here, we want to be informed of such an event in order to be able to show the remote video on our web page:

```
pc.onaddstream = onRemoteStreamAdded;
```

If the establishment of the connection fails, we will get an exception. Here, you can add debug console logging and UI improvements to inform the customer that something is wrong:

```
    } catch (e) {
        pc = null;
        return;
    }
};
```

When we have ICE candidates from the WebRTC API, we want to send them to the remote peer in order to establish a connection:

```
function onIceCandidate(event) {
    if (event.candidate)
```

```
        sendMessage({type: 'candidate', label: event.candidate.
    sdpMLineIndex, id: event.candidate.sdpMid,
            candidate: event.candidate.candidate});
    };
```

We will get trapped into this function when a direct connection has been established and a remote peer has added its media stream to the connection. We want to show a remote video so, here, we're attaching a remote video to the video tag on the web page:

```
function onRemoteStreamAdded(event) {
    attachMediaStream(remoteVideo, event.stream);
```

We also want to store a reference to the remote stream in order to use it later:

```
    remoteStream = event.stream;
};
```

The following function is called by us when we're joining a virtual room and initiating a call to the remote peer:

```
function doCall() {
```

We don't want to use the data channel yet (as it will be introduced in the next chapter). It is enabled in Firefox by default so here, we're asking Firefox to disable it:

```
    var constraints = {"optional": [], "mandatory":
    {"MozDontOfferDataChannel": true}};
```

Check whether we're running this execution under Chrome and if so, remove the unnecessary options that are preconfigured to run under Firefox:

```
    if (webrtcDetectedBrowser === "chrome")
        for (var prop in constraints.mandatory) if (prop.
    indexOf("Moz") != -1) delete constraints.mandatory[prop];
```

Merge browser options with the whole constraints entity, and call the createOffer function in order to initiate a peer connection. In case of a success, we will get into the setLocalAndSendMessage function:

```
    constraints = mergeConstraints(constraints, sdpConstraints);
    pc.createOffer(setLocalAndSendMessage, null, constraints);
};
```

If we're waiting for a call and have got an offer from a remote peer, we need to answer the call in order to establish a connection and begin the conference.

Here is the function that will be used to answer a call. As is the case with `doAnswer`, we will get into the `setLocalAndSendMessage` function in case of a success:

```
function doAnswer() {
    pc.createAnswer(setLocalAndSendMessage, null, sdpConstraints);
};
```

The preceding callback function is used during the process of establishing a connection by the WebRTC API. We receive a session description entity, and then we need to set up a local description and send an SDP object to the remote peer via a signaling server:

```
function setLocalAndSendMessage(sessionDescription) {
    pc.setLocalDescription(sessionDescription);
    sendMessage(sessionDescription);
};
```

The following is a simple helper that merges the constraints:

```
function mergeConstraints(cons1, cons2) {
    var merged = cons1;
    for (var name in cons2.mandatory) merged.mandatory[name] =
cons2.mandatory[name];
    merged.optional.concat(cons2.optional);
    return merged;
};
```

Developing an index page

We have two JavaScript files under our www directory: `myrtclib.js` and `myrtcadapter.js`.

Now, it's time to use them and create an index page of the application.

Create an index page file, www/`index.html`:

```
<!DOCTYPE html>
<html>
<head>
    <title>My WebRTC application</title>
```

Here, we defined a style for the page to place a local and remote video object one by one on the same row:

```
<style type="text/css">
section {
    width: 90%;
```

```
        height: 200px;
        background: red;
        margin: auto;
        padding: 10px;
    }
    div#lVideo {
        width: 45%;
        height: 200px;
        background: black;
        float: left;
    }
    div#rVideo {
        margin-left: 45%;
        height: 200px;
        background: black;
    }
    </style>
```

Include our adapter and wrapper JavaScript code:

```
<script type="text/javascript"src="myrtclib.js"></script>
<script type="text/javascript"src="myrtcadapter.js"></script>
</head>
```

We want to perform some additional actions after the page is loaded, but before the start of the conferencing, we use the onLoad property of the body HTML tag to call the appropriate function:

```
<body onLoad="onPageLoad();">
```

The status div will be used to store the information about the customer. For example, we will put a URL there with a virtual room number that is to be shared between the peers:

```
<div id='status'></div>
<section>
```

Local and remote video objects

We use the autoplay option to start the video streaming automatically after the media stream has been attached.

We mute the local video object in order to avoid the local echo effect:

```
<div id='lVideo'>
    <video width="100%" height="100%"autoplay="autoplay"
id="localVideo" muted="true"></video>
```

```
</div>
<div id='rVideo'>
    <video width="100%" height="100%"autoplay="autoplay"
id="remoteVideo"></video>
</div>
</section>
```

The following function will be called by the web browser after the page has been loaded:

```
<script>
function onPageLoad() {
```

First of all, we will try to make the UI look nicer. Here, we try to get the width of every video object and set an appropriate height parameter. We assume that the width/height is 4/3 and calculate the height for each object respectively:

```
var _divV = document.getElementById("lVideo");
var _w = _divV.offsetWidth;
var _h = _w * 3 / 4;
_divV.offsetHeight = _h;
_divV.setAttribute("style","height:"+_h+"px");
_divV.style.height=_h+'px';

_divV = document.getElementById("rVideo");
_divV.setAttribute("style","height:"+_h+"px");
_divV.style.height=_h+'px';
```

This is the main point where we start our conference. We pass the signaling server's URL and local/remote objects' references to the initialization function, and the magic begins.

Please use appropriate IP address and port values where your signaling server is running (we will begin to build it in the next page):

```
myrtclibinit("ws://IP:PORT",document.getElementById("localVideo"),docu
ment.getElementById("remoteVideo"));
};
```

This is a callback function called from our `myrtclib.js` script when the signaling server returns a virtual room's number. Here, we construct an appropriate URL for our customer to share it with a friend:

```
function OnRoomReceived(room) {
  var st = document.getElementById("status");
```

```
    st.innerHTML = "Now, if somebody wants to join you, should use this
link: <a href=\""+window.location.href+"?room="+room+"\">"+window.
location.href+"?room="+room+"</a>";
};
</script>
</body>
</html>
```

A simple p2p video conference – the server application

We prepared a client-side code to be executed inside a web browser. Now it is time to develop the signaling server. As a transport layer for the signaling mechanism, we will use WebSockets; it is supported well by all web browsers that support WebRTC, and this protocol is pretty suitable for the signaling role.

The application description file

The application description file describes our application. It is something similar to the manifest file for C# applications or Java applets. Here, we describe what our application itself is, define its version number, define other modules it depends on, and so on.

Edit the apps/rtcserver/src/rtcserver.app.src file.

The application ID/name is as follows:

```
{application, rtcserver,
  [
```

The application description is not mandatory, so for now, we can skip it. The version number is set to 1 as we have just started. The applications option gives a list of applications that we depend on. We also define the main module's name and environment variables (empty list):

```
{description, ""},
{vsn, "1"},
{registered, []},
{applications, [
                kernel,
                stdlib,
                cowlib,
                cowboy,
                compiler,
```

```
                gproc
            ]},
    {mod, { rtcserver_app, []}},
    {env, []}
]}.
```

The application module

This application module is the main module of our signaling server application. Here, we start all the applications we're depending on and set up a web server and WebSocket handler for it.

Edit the `apps/rtcserver/src/rtcserver_app.erl` the file.

The module name should be the same as the file name:

```
-module(rtcserver_app).
```

We tell Erlang VM that this is an application module:

```
-behaviour(application).
```

Describe which functions should be accessible from this module; `/2`, `/1`, and `/0` are the parities of the function, that is, the number of arguments:

```
-export([start/2, stop/1, start/0]).
```

Now we need to start all the helping applications that we're depending on and then start our application itself:

```
start() ->
    ok = application:start(compiler),
```

Ranch is an effective connection pool:

```
    ok = application:start(ranch),
```

Crypto needs to support SSL:

```
    ok = application:start(crypto),
```

Cowboy is a lightweight web server that we use to build our signaling server on WebSockets:

```
    ok = application:start(cowlib),
    ok = application:start(cowboy),
```

We use `gproc` as a simple key/value DB in the memory to store the virtual rooms' numbers:

```
ok = application:start(gproc),
```

Start our application:

```
ok = application:start(rtcserver).
```

The following function will be called during the process of starting the application:

```
start(_StartType, _StartArgs) ->
```

First of all, we define a dispatcher, an entity used by the Cowboy application. With the dispatcher, we tell Cowboy where it should listen for requests from the clients and how to map requests to handlers:

```
Dispatch = cowboy_router:compile([
                                {'_',[
```

Here, we define that every /* request to our signaling server should be processed by the `handler_websocket` module (will be reviewed on the following page):

```
{"/", handler_websocket, []}
]}
]),
```

Here, we ask Cowboy to start listening and processing clients' requests. Our HTTP process is named `websocket`; it should listen on port `30000` and bind to any available network interface(s). The connection timeout value is set to `500` ms and the `max_keep_alive` timeout is set to `50` seconds:

```
{ok, _} = cowboy:start_http(websocket, 100, [{port, 30000}], [{env,
[{dispatch, Dispatch}]},
{max_keepalive, 50},
{timeout, 500}
]),
```

To make our application work, we need to call the `start_link` function of the application's supervisor:

```
rtcserver_sup:start_link().
```

The following function is called when we want to stop the signaling server:

```
stop(_State) ->
    ok.
```

The server supervisor

To make our Erlang-based signaling server work properly, we need to implement a supervisor process. This is the standard way in which Erlang applications usually work. This is not something specific to WebRTC applications, so we won't dive into deep details here. The code is very short.

Edit the `apps/rtcserver/src/rtcserver_sup.erl` file:

```
-module(rtcserver_sup).
-behaviour(supervisor).
-export([start_link/0]).
-export([init/1]).

-define(CHILD(I, Type), {I, {I, start_link, []}, permanent, 5000,
Type, [I]}).

start_link() ->
    supervisor:start_link({local, ?MODULE}, ?MODULE, []).

init([]) ->
    {ok, { {one_for_one, 5, 10}, []} }.
```

The WebSocket handler

A WebSocket handler module will implement the signaling server's functionality. It will communicate with both the peers, create rooms, and do all the other stuff that we're awaiting to get done from the signaling server.

Edit the `apps/rtcserver/src/handler_websocket.erl` file:

```
-module(handler_websocket).
-behaviour(cowboy_websocket_handler).
-export([init/3]).
-export([websocket_init/3, websocket_handle/3,
         websocket_info/3, websocket_terminate/3]).
```

The following is a record where we can store useful information about the connection and peers:

```
-record(state, {
        client = undefined :: undefined | binary(),
        state = undefined :: undefined | connected | running,
        room = undefined :: undefined | integer()
}).
```

We're trapped here when a peer tries to connect to the signaling server. At this stage, we just need to reply with the upgrade state to establish the WebSockets connection with the web browser properly:

```
init(_Any, _Req, _Opt) ->
    {upgrade, protocol, cowboy_websocket}.
```

The following function is called when the connection is established (a peer has been connected to the signaling server):

```
websocket_init(_TransportName, Req, _Opt) ->
```

Get the x-forwarded-for field from HTTP request header, and store it as the peer's IP address:

```
{Client, Req1} = cowboy_req:header(<<"x-forwarded-for">>, Req),
State = #state{client = Client, state = connected},
{ok, Req1, State, hibernate}.
```

The following function is called when we get a message from some of our peers. We need to parse the message, decide what to do, and reply if necessary:

```
websocket_handle({text,Data}, Req, State) ->
```

Mark our state as running; the new peer is connected and the peer to signaling server connection has been established:

```
StateNew = case (State#state.state) of
                    started ->
State#state{state = running};
                _ ->
                    State
            end,
```

We use JSON to encode messages that are transferred between the clients and the signaling server, so we need to decode the message:

```
JSON = jsonerl:decode(Data),
    {M,Type} = element(1,JSON),    case M of
<<"type">> ->
            case Type of
```

The type of the message is GETROOM; someone wants to create a virtual room. Here, we will create the room and reply with the room's number:

```
<<"GETROOM">> ->
```

We use the `generate_room` function to create a virtual room:

```
Room = generate_room(),
```

Construct the answer message and encode it to JSON:

```
R = iolist_to_binary(jsonerl:encode({{type, <<"GETROOM">>}, {value,
Room}})),
```

Store the room number and the associated process ID in the key/value DB.
If someone tries to enter a virtual room, we need some mechanism to understand
whether the room exists:

```
gproc:reg({p,l, Room}),
```

Store the room number in the `state` entity; we will want to reuse this value
further on:

```
S = (StateNew#state{room = Room}),
```

Send our reply back to the peer and exit:

```
{reply, {text, <<R/binary>>}, Req, S, hibernate};
```

If the message type is ENTERROOM, it means that someone tries to enter a virtual room
that does exist and someone has to be present in this room already:

```
<<"ENTERROOM">> ->
```

Extract the room number from the message and look up all the participants present
in the virtual room:

```
{<<"value">>,Room} = element(2,JSON),                        Participants
= gproc:lookup_pids({p,l,Room}),
                    case length(Participants) of
```

If we have just one participant, register the new peer process ID in this room and
store the room number in the `state` entity:

```
1 ->
    gproc:reg({p,l, Room}),
    S = (StateNew#state{room = Room}),
    {ok, Req, S, hibernate};
```

Otherwise, reply with the WRONGROOM message back to the peer:

```
_ ->
R = iolist_to_binary(jsonerl:encode({{type, <<"WRONGROOM">>}})),
{reply, {text, <<R/binary>>}, Req, StateNew, hibernate}
    end;
```

If we get a message of some other type, then just transfer it to connected peer:

```
            _ ->
    reply2peer(Data, StateNew#state.room),
                    {ok, Req, StateNew, hibernate}
            end;
        _ ->
            reply2peer(Data, State#state.room),
            {ok, Req, StateNew, hibernate}
    end;
```

If we get a message of an unknown sort, we just ignore it:

```
    websocket_handle(_Any, Req, State) ->
        {ok, Req, State, hibernate}.
```

The preceding method is called when we receive a message from the other process; in this case, we send the message to the connected peer. We will use the following code to implement the web chat and data transfer functionality in later chapters:

```
    websocket_info(_Info, Req, State) ->
        {reply, {text,_Info}, Req, State, hibernate}.
```

The following code is called when the connection is terminated (the remote peer closed the web browser, for example):

```
    websocket_terminate(_Reason, _Req, _State) ->
        ok.
```

Send a message (R) to every peer that is connected to the room except the one we received the message from:

```
    reply2peer(R, Room) ->
        [P ! <<R/binary>> || P <- gproc:lookup_pids({p,l,Room}) --
    [self()]].
```

Generate the virtual room number using a random number generator:

```
    generate_room() ->
        random:seed(now()),
        random:uniform(999999).
```

Developing a configuration script for Rebar

We need to tell the Rebar tool which applications our server is dependent on and where we can download them.

Edit the `apps/rtcserver/rebar.config` file:

```
{erl_opts, [warnings_as_errors]}.
{deps,
[
{'gproc', ".*", {
git, "git://github.com/esl/gproc.git", {tag, "0.2.16"}
}},
{'jsonerl', ".*", {
git, "git://github.com/fycth/jsonerl.git", "master"
}},
{'cowboy', ".*", {
git,"https://github.com/extend/cowboy.git","0.9.0"
}} ]}.
```

Compiling and running the signaling server

Create another `rebar.config` file under your project's folder:

```
{sub_dirs, [
    "apps/rtcserver"
]}.
```

This configuration file tells the Rebar tool that it needs to look into `apps/rtcserver` and process the content.

Now, go to the project's directory and execute the following command in the console:

rebar get-deps

It will download all the necessary dependencies to the `deps` directory.

We want to compile our code, so we execute the following command:

rebar compile

It will compile our application and dependencies. After this gets completed, start the `rtcserver` application using the following command:

erl -pa deps/*/ebin apps/*/ebin -saslerrlog_type error -s rtcserver_app

Using this command, you will get into the Erlang VM console and start the signaling server (the `rtcserver` application). From now on, it will listen on the TCP port `30000` (or the other one, if you changed it in the code).

You can check where the server is listening on the requests using the `netstat` command. For Linux, you can use the following command:

```
netstat -na | grep 30000
```

If the server is running, you should see it listening on the port that is binded to the `0.0.0.0` address.

For Windows, you can use the following construction:

```
netstat -na | findstr 30000
```

Let's start the conference!

We started the signaling server and now it is time to test our application. Now, point your web browser to the domain you prepared for your application. It should open the index page with your web camera's view on it. Above the camera's view, you should see the URL that will direct the second participant to join the conference. Open this URL on another machine, and the connection should establish automatically and both sides should be able to see each other's videos.

To stop the signaling server and quit from VM console, you can use the `q().` command.

Configuring and installing your own STUN server

As you already know, it is important to have access to the STUN/TURN server to work with peers located behind NAT or a firewall. In this chapter, developing our application, we used pubic STUN servers (actually, they are public Google servers accessible from other networks).

Nevertheless, if you plan to build your own service, you should install your own STUN/TURN server. This way, your application will not be dependent on a server even you can't control. Today, we have public STUN servers from Google; tomorrow, they can be switched off. So, the right way is to have your own STUN/TURN server.

In this section, you will be introduced to installing the STUN server as a simpler case. The installation and configuration of the TURN server is more complex and will be discovered in *Chapter 4, Security and Authentication*, during the development of another application.

There are several implementations of STUN servers that you can find on the Internet. You can take this one: `http://www.stunprotocol.org`.

The server is cross-platform and can be used under Windows, Mac OS X, or Linux.

To start the STUN server, you should use the following command line:

```
stunserver --mode full --primaryinterfacex1.x1.x1.x1 --altinterfacex2.
x2.x2.x2
```

Please pay attention to the fact that you need two IP addresses on your machine to run the STUN server. It is mandatory in order to make the STUN protocol work correctly. The machine can have only one physical network interface, but it should also have a network alias with an IP address that is different from the one we used on the main network interface.

Summary

In this chapter, we developed a video conference service using WebRTC. During the development process, we learned what STUN and TURN servers are and how they can help us achieve our goals. We got an introduction to the main WebRTC API functions. Now you know what we mean by keywords such as ICE and SDP and why they are very useful.

You also had a chance to get acquainted with Erlang and WebSockets, if you were not already acquainted with them.

In the next chapter, we will learn what Data API is and will develop a peer-to-peer file-sharing application. Most of the keywords and code will be not new for you, so it will be easier to get to the topic.

Using the WebRTC Data API

2

This chapter introduces the Data API topic of the WebRTC technology. You will learn what the Data API is and how to use it to develop rich media applications. For practice, we will develop a simple, peer-to-peer file sharing application. You will also get a brief introduction on using the HTML5 File API.

Introducing the Data API

The WebRTC Data API introduces the RTCDataChannel entity, which enables direct data connections between peers (just like for audio and video media channels), as we learned in *Chapter1*, *Developing a WebRTC Application*.

Used in pair with RTCPeerConnection and utilizing the ICE framework, it makes it possible to link up direct data connections through firewalls and NATs. The Data API can be used to build powerful, low-latency applications such as games, remote desktops, desktop sharing, real-time private text chats, peer-to-peer file sharing, and torrents.

Data channels in WebRTC have built-in security. They are usually even faster than WebSocket connections (browser-to-server), because connections proceed between browsers without any point in the middle. Nevertheless, if you turn on the server, data will be transmitted via the server (consuming additional bandwidth on the server side). Also, connection establishment using data channels takes longer than when using WebSockets, because of the additional actions that are needed.

Using data channels is as simple as using WebSocket channels. Data channels can be used in parallel with audio and video channels between the same peers. Text or binary data can be transmitted using data channels.

Data channels can be reliable or unreliable. Reliable channels are similar to TCP connections; the messages that you have sent will be transmitted to the other side and in the same order. On the other hand, unreliable channels are more like UDP connections; there is no guarantee that all your messages will be delivered and that they will arrive in any particular order.

Introducing protocols

In general, WebRTC implements the following set of data channel protocols:

- **Secure Real-time Transport Protocol (SRTP)**: This is used for exchanging with media such as audio and video

- **Secure Real-time Control Transport Protocol (SRTCP)**: This is used for exchanging with statistics and control data for an SRTP connection

- **Stream Control Transmission Protocol (SCTP)**: This is used for exchanging with non-media data

Kindly note, SRTP is a secured version of **RTP (Real-time Transport Protocol)**. The WebRTC standard requires that all data exchanges should be secured. So, working on our applications we will learn and use secured protocols only.

As you can see, in this chapter, we will use the SCTP protocol to develop our application. SCTP runs over DTLS, and DTLS runs over UDP.

It is possible to configure reliability and the message order using the DataChannel API, as follows:

- In-order or out-of-order delivery of messages
- Reliable or partially reliable delivery of messages

Configuring partial reliability is also possible using the following two different policies:

- Partially reliable delivery with retransmission: In this case, messages will not be retransmitted more than the specified number of times by the application

- Partially reliable delivery with timeout: In this case, messages will not be retransmitted after a specified lifetime (in milliseconds) by the application

Each data channel can be configured individually. Data channels used by peers are independent of each other.

Introducing HTML5

In this book, we will use the HTML5 API to perform different tasks with JavaScript while developing our demo applications.

HTML5 itself is the latest standard for HTML and you can find its home page at `http://www.w3.org/TR/html5/`.

Its ancestor HTML 4.01 came in 1999, and the Internet has changed significantly since then. HTML5 was designed to deliver rich content without the need for additional plugins. The current version delivers everything, from animation to graphics, music to movies, and can also be used to build complicated web applications.

HTML5 is also designed to be cross-platform. It is designed to work irrespective of whether you are using a PC, a Tablet, a Smartphone, or a Smart TV.

We will use HTML5 while working on our WebRTC applications; in this chapter, we will start with the HTML5 File API.

Introducing the HTML5 File API

Data channels help us to transmit data (files) between peers. Nevertheless, it doesn't provide any mechanism to read and write files. So, we need some mechanism to be able to read/write files.

For the purpose of filesystem access, we will use the HTML5 File API. It provides a standard way to interact with local files. Using this API, you can create and read files, create thumbnails for image files, save application preferences, and more. You can also verify on the client side; if a customer wants to upload the MIME type of file, you can restrict the uploading by the file size.

When reading files, we will use the `FileReader` object. It reads files asynchronously and provides the following four ways (methods) to read them:

- `readAsBinaryString`: This will read a file into a binary string. Every byte is represented by an integer in the range from 0 to 255.

- `readAsText`: This reads the file as a text string. By default, the result string is decoded as UTF-8. You can use the optional encoding parameter to specify a different format.

- `readAsDataURL`: This reads the file's content and encodes it to DataURL. In our application, we will use this method to read files selected by the customer.

- `readAsArrayBuffer`: This reads the file's content to the `ArrayBuffer` object.

Known limitations

WebRTC and its Data API are supported by major web browsers. Nevertheless, the WebRTC standard is not yet complete and web browsers can still behave in different ways.

Chrome versions lower than 31 uses the RTP data channel type by default; Firefox uses SCTP by default in all versions.

At the time of writing these lines, Chrome still has some traits in the data channel's implementation. They limit channel bandwidth, which can cause unexpected effects. To fix it, you can use a hack described in this chapter.

With some browsers (not having fully compliant support of the WebRTC API), you can face the unexpected behavior while transmitting big-sized files that cause weird errors.

Nevertheless, all these cases are temporary. You can check the current status of the data channel's implementation on the WebRTC home page at `http://www.webrtc.org/home`.

Also, you can check the browser's home page for more detailed information on supporting the WebRTC API for a particular browser's version.

Preparing the environment

The whole structure of our application will be the same as in the previous chapter.

We need to create a folder for the new application, for example, `filesharing_app`. Again, create a subfolder for the HTML/JavaScript part, for example, `filesharing_app/www`.

We still need a signaling server, and in this chapter we won't introduce any new functionality on the server side. So, you can take the signaling server from the previous chapter. It will work fine for the new application that we're going to develop. You can just copy the signaling server from `my_rtc_project/apps/rtcserver` and paste it to `filesharing_app/apps/`.

We will also need the WebRTC API JavaScript adapter that we developed in the previous chapter. The adapter library can be used from the previous chapter with no change, so we need not pay much attention to it in this chapter.

So, take the signaling server application and the `myrtcadapter.js` library from the application we developed in the previous chapter.

A simple file-sharing service – the browser application

The client code of our new application is very similar to the previous application in some parts. Nevertheless, it will be significantly different in the core side, so we will rework it and discuss it in detail in this chapter.

The WebRTC API wrapper

We developed a wrapper for the WebRTC API in the previous chapter, so now it will be even easier to do the same for our new application. Now we will add some new code relevant to the Data API and for HTML5-specific API functions, which will be useful for file I/O operations, by performing the following steps:

1. Create the www/myrtclib.js file as we already did in *Chapter 1, Developing a WebRTC Application*. We need to declare an entity to control the WebRTC peer connection API. Using the myrtcadapter.js library, we will detect the browser type and version, and assign a relevant API function to this entity.

2. We also need to detect the web browser's version in order to handle it appropriately by using the following code:

   ```
   var RTCPeerConnection = null;
   var webrtcDetectedBrowser = null;
   ```

3. We need to handle the room number and initiator flag, as in the previous application, in order to know the virtual room number and if we are waiting for a call or we want to make one. This can be done using the following code:

   ```
   var room = null;
   var initiator;
   ```

4. This step is identical to the one in the previous chapter. We declare variables to control the signaling channel and its state, the peer connection, and the signaling URL (we use it to communicate with our signaling server), as shown in the following code:

   ```
   var channelReady;
   var channel;
   var pc = null;
   var signalingURL;
   ```

5. The following are the new variables that we are introducing in this chapter. We need them to control the data channels that we will create between peers. We will declare them as follows:

```
var sendDChannel = null;
var recvDChannel = null;
```

We declared two constraint variables, one for the peer connection and the other for the data channel.

6. As we discussed before, there are two major data channel types: RTP and SCTP. We will try to detect the browser version and use the relevant connection type.

7. We will define `pc_constraints` to switch to using the RTP channel (we will pass `null` to the WebRTC API in case we want to use SCTP).

8. We also declare the `data_constraint` variable. By default, SCTP channels are unreliable and RTP ones are reliable. So, in case we are using RTP channels, we need to indicate our need for an unreliable channel by using the following code:

```
var pc_constraints = {"optional": [{RtpDataChannels: true}]};
var data_constraint = {reliable :false};
```

9. We need the set of STUN/TURN servers (as you remember from the previous chapter) to pass through firewalls and NAT as follows:

```
var pc_config = {"iceServers":
    [{url:'stun:23.21.150.121'},
    {url:'stun:stun.1.google.com:19302'}]};
```

10. Now, we will do some preparations and initializations of the WebRTC API with the following in our initialization function:

```
function myrtclibinit(sURL) {
```

11. We still need to know the URL of our signaling server and initialize the `myrtcadapter.js` library, as we did in the video conference application, as follows:

```
signalingURL = sURL;
initWebRTCAdapter();
```

This is something new; we want to know a little about the web browser under which we're running our application.

12. If we have Firefox, we want it to use the SCTP data channel type. If we have a Chrome version that is greater than or equal to Version 31, we also want to use SCTP. For any other browser, we will try to use the RTP data channel implementation. This can be done using the following code:

```
if (webrtcDetectedBrowser === 'firefox' ||
    (webrtcDetectedBrowser === 'chrome' &&
webrtcDetectedVersion >= 31)) {
```

13. Before we declare constraints for the peer connection and data channel to use them with the RTP data channel type, for Firefox and Chrome higher than or equal to Version 31, we will make them equal to `null`, as shown in the following code (in this case, we're asking the browser to use SCTP instead of RTP):

```
pc_constraints = null;
data_constraint = null;
openChannel();
}
```

14. The following function opens a connection channel to the signaling server:

```
function openChannel() {
    channelReady = false;
    channel = new WebSocket(signalingURL);
    channel.onopen = onChannelOpened;
    channel.onmessage = onChannelMessage;
    channel.onclose = onChannelClosed;
};
```

15. We will use the following function, exactly as it appeared in the video conference service with only a minor change related to creating a data channel:

```
function onChannelOpened() {
    channelReady = true;
    createPeerConnection();

    if(location.search.substring(1,5) == "room") {
        room = location.search.substring(6);
        sendMessage({"type" : "ENTERROOM", "value" : room *
1});
        initiator = true;
        doCall();
    } else {
        sendMessage({"type" : "GETROOM", "value" :""});
        initiator = false;
    }
};
```

16. When we receive a message from the signaling server, we still need to process it and react on it, by using the following code:

```
function onChannelMessage(message) {
    processSignalingMessage(message.data);
};
```

17. We need to indicate that the signaling channel is closed when the connection to the signaling server is lost. This can be done by using the following code:

```
function onChannelClosed() {
    channelReady = false;
};
```

18. Using the following function, we will communicate to the other peers using the signaling server:

```
function sendMessage(message) {
    var msgString = JSON.stringify(message);
    channel.send(msgString);
};
```

19. Now that this is done, we need to parse and process messages received from the signaling server or other peers and react on the messages. There won't be many changes here; the whole connection and interoperation mechanism remains the same. The following function will parse the received message, check its type, and call the appropriate code:

```
function processSignalingMessage(message) {
    var msg = JSON.parse(message);

    if (msg.type === 'offer') {
        pc.setRemoteDescription(new
RTCSessionDescription(msg));
        doAnswer();
    } else if (msg.type === 'answer') {
        pc.setRemoteDescription(new
RTCSessionDescription(msg));
    } else if (msg.type === 'candidate') {
        var candidate = new RTCIceCandidate({sdpMLineIndex:m
sg.label, candidate:msg.candidate});
        pc.addIceCandidate(candidate);
    } else if (msg.type === 'GETROOM') {
        room = msg.value;
        OnRoomReceived(room);
    } else if (msg.type === 'WRONGROOM') {
        window.location.href = "/";
    }
};
```

20. Now, we need to create a new peer connection. We have it from the previous application; however, in this chapter, it has a slightly different logic, and we haven't declared the constraints for the peer connection yet. We have declared the constraints before. At this stage, constraints will be equal to `null` or the RTP option, depending on the browser we're running under. The following function will create a peer connection object and assign appropriate event handlers for it:

```
function createPeerConnection() {
    try {
        pc = new RTCPeerConnection(pc_config, pc_constraints);
        pc.onicecandidate = onIceCandidate;
        pc.ondatachannel = recvChannelCallback;
    } catch (e) {
        console.log(e);
        pc = null;
        return;
    }
};
```

21. The following function is a new function to create a new data channel:

```
function createDataChannel(role) {
```

22. Create a new data channel. We pass its name constructed from the virtual room number and the `mydatachannel` word. You can use any channel name you like.

23. The second parameter of the create function uses data constraints. According to the logic discussed previously, for Firefox and Chrome higher than or equal to Version 31 data constraints will be equal to `null` because we want to use the SCTP connection type for these browsers.

```
try {
sendDChannel = pc.createDataChannel("datachannel_"+room+role,
data_constraint); } catch (e) {
        console.log('error creating data channel ' + e);
        return;
    }
```

24. Using the following code, we assign callback functions to handle onchannel open and onchannel close events:

```
        sendDChannel.onopen = onSendChannelStateChange;
        sendDChannel.onclose = onSendChannelStateChange;
};
```

25. We took the following function from our video conference application; we need this and can use it unchanged.

```
function onIceCandidate(event) {
        if (event.candidate)
             sendMessage({type: candidate, label: event.candidate.
sdpMLineIndex, id: event.candidate.sdpMid,
                candidate: event.candidate.candidate});
        };
```

26. The following is a callback function. It is called by the `createOffer` and the `createAnswer` functions. It will be called if something wrong happens during creating a call or answering the call.

```
function failureCallback(e) {
        console.log("failure callback "+ e.message);
}
```

27. The following is the `doCall` function, which is very similar to the one we used in the previous chapter:

```
function doCall() {
```

28. The only major change here is that we need to create a data channel before we actually call. The `createdataChannel` function is called from here when we want to make a call, and we call it from the `processSignalingMessage` function when we're waiting for an incoming call. As you can see, we also pass the caller parameter to the function when creating a new data channel. This name will be used as an identifier for the newly created data channel. After we create a new data channel, we also need to create an offer for the remote peer for establishing connection.

```
        createDataChannel("caller");        pc.createOffer(setLocalAnd
SendMessage, failureCallback, null);
        };
```

29. The following function is called when we want to receive a call:

```
function doAnswer() {
     pc.createAnswer(setLocalAndSendMessage, failureCallback,
null);
        };
```

30. The following is the function for handling session descriptions, and it is very similar to the one we used for our video conference service:

```
function setLocalAndSendMessage(sessionDescription) {
```

31. For this application, we need to implement a little hack to make it work well. By default, Chrome has the bandwidth limitation option declared in the `sessionDescription` entity when we create it. It can lead to weird issues during file transmission.

32. What we want to do here is remove such bandwidth limitation options from the SDP entity. This functionality is implemented in the `bandwidthHack` function as follows:

```
        sessionDescription.sdp = bandwidthHack(sessionDescription.
sdp);
        pc.setLocalDescription(sessionDescription);
        sendMessage(sessionDescription);
    };
```

33. Here is the dirty hack. We took the SDP entity and removed the bandwidth limitation options from it. Probably, in future, the JavaScript API will be implemented to control SDP objects and its options. Today, we need to invent some kind of dirty hack and patch session description objects directly.

34. You can refer to RFC on the session description protocol to understand which options it can have and how you can change them, at `http://www.ietf.org/rfc/rfc2327.txt`.

```
        function bandwidthHack(sdp) {
```

Firefox doesn't have such issues, so we don't have to make any changes to the `sdp` entity if we're running under Firefox, as shown in the following code:

```
        if (webrtcDetectedBrowser === 'firefox') return sdp;
```

In general, we want to remove any `b=AS` fields from the SDP. You can get more technical details on this parameter of the SDP protocol in the appropriate RFC at `http://www.rfc-editor.org/rfc/rfc3556.txt`. The following piece of code will remove the bandwidth option from the SDP packet using a regular expression:

```
        sdp = sdp.replace( /b=AS([^\r\n]+\r\n)/g , '');
```

We can remove them or we can try to extend the bandwidth limit, as shown in the following code:

```
sdp=sdp.replace(/a=mid:data\r\n/g, 'a=mid:data\r\nb=AS:1638400\
r\n');

        return sdp;
    };
```

35. The following function is called from UI side (`index.html`) when we want to send data to the peer:

```
function sendDataMessage(data) {
    sendDChannel.send(data);
};
```

36. The following function represents a callback function that will be called when the status of a data channel has been changed. What we're doing here is detecting if the state has been changed to open; if so, we assign an appropriate callback function to the channel in order to handle the onmessage receive event, as shown in the following code:

```
function onSendChannelStateChange() {
console.log('Send channel state is: ' + sendDChannel.readyState);
        if (sendDChannel.readyState === 'open') sendDChannel.
onmessage = onReceiveMessageCallback;
    }
```

37. We also need to implement a callback function for our receiver channel. In the following code, we will assign an appropriate event handler for the channel:

```
function recvChannelCallback(evt) {
        console.log('Receive Channel Callback');
        recvDChannel = evt.channel;
        recvDChannel.onmessage = onReceiveMessageCallback;
        recvDChannel.onopen = onReceiveChannelStateChange;
        recvDChannel.onclose = onReceiveChannelStateChange;
}
```

38. The following is a callback function and it is called when "receiver channel" is opened. Logically, we have two data channels, but technically these two data channels are one. So, here we make `sendDChannel` and `recvDChannel` equal, as shown in the following code:

```
    function onReceiveChannelStateChange() {
console.log('Receive channel state is: ' + recvDChannel.
readyState);
if (recvDChannel.readyState === 'open') sendDChannel =
recvDChannel;
    }
```

39. The following callback function is used to receive data from the remote peer. Here we parse the received message; in case this is a part of the transmitted file, we call an appropriate handler that will collect the received binary data.

```
function onReceiveMessageCallback(event) {
        try {
```

```
            var msg = JSON.parse(event.data);
            if (msg.type === 'file')
            {
                onFileReceived(msg.name, msg.size, msg.data);
            }
        }
        catch (e) {}
    };
```

Developing the main page of the application

As we did in the previous *Chapter 1, Developing a WebRTC Application*, we need an `index.html` page where we will implement the UI visible for customers and some additional JavaScript code to implement the client application. This can be done by performing the following steps:

1. Create the index page at `www/index.html` as follows:

```
<!DOCTYPE html>
<html>
<head>
    <title>My WebRTC file sharing application</title>
<style type="text/css">
```

2. Include the following two JavaScript libraries:

```
</style>
    <script type="text/javascript" src="myrtclib.js"></script>
    <script type="text/javascript" src="myrtcadapter.js"></script>
</head>

<body onLoad="onPageLoad();">
<div id='status'></div>
```

3. Using this object, we will handle the list of files chosen by the customer. Using this list, we will send files one by one to the peer by using the following code:

```
<div>
    <input type="file" id="files" name="files[]" multiple />
    <output id="list"></output>
</div>
```

4. After selecting the files to send, the user has to click on the **Send** button given in the following code:

```
<div>
    <button onclick="onSendBtnClick()">Send</button>
</div>
```

5. We need to store a reference to the `filelist` object, as shown in the following code:

```
<script>
    var filelist;

function onPageLoad() {
```

6. We need to know if the web browser supports the HTML5 File API by using the following code:

```
    if (window.File && window.FileReader && window.FileList &&
window.Blob) {
    } else {
        alert('The File APIs are not fully supported in this
browser.');
        return;
    }
```

7. Get the `files` object and add an event listener to it, as shown in the following code. This way, we will let the customer choose the file(s) to send.

```
    document.getElementById('files').addEventListener('change',
handleFileSelect, false);
```

8. Now, we can initialize our WebRTC API wrapper library that we developed previously. As in the previous chapter, you have to pass the domain name or IP address on which the signaling server is running and the port, as shown in the following code:

```
    myrtclibinit("ws://<DOMAIN_OR_IP>:<PORT>");
};
```

9. The following function is called when the customer clicks on the **Send** button:

```
function onSendBtnClick() {
```

10. Go through the `filelist` variable and take files one by one, as shown in the following code:

```
    for (var i = 0, f; f = filelist[i]; i++) {
```

11. Create a `FileReader` object of the HTML5 File API to read a file's content as follows:

```
var reader = new FileReader();
```

12. We need to assign a callback function to the `FileReader` object; it will be called when the file is loaded, as shown in the following code:

```
reader.onload = (function(theFile) {
    return function(evt) {
```

13. We will send files packed inside a JSON structure with the metadata attached: the filename and size. So, here we will construct a new JSON object and prepare it to be sent to the peer, using the following code:

```
var msg = JSON.stringify({"type" : "file", "name"
: theFile.name, "size" : theFile.size, "data" : evt.target.
result});
```

14. Now, we call our function declared in the `myrtclib.js` library and pass the structure to send it, using the following code:

```
sendDataMessage(msg);
        };
    })(f);
```

15. Kindly note that the preceding function was the `FileReader` callback function and here is where we start the process. We call the `readAsDataURL` method of the `FileReader` object. After that, the browser will try to read file; we will get into our previous callback function and send the file to the peer, as shown in the following code:

```
reader.readAsDataURL(f);
    }
};
```

This is a callback function called when we receive the virtual room number from the signaling server.

16. The only thing we need to do here is show the room URL to the customer using the `status` div object, as shown in the following code:

```
function OnRoomReceived(room) {
    var st = document.getElementById("status");
    st.innerHTML = "Now, if somebody wants to join you,
should use this link: <a href=\""+window.location.
href+"?room="+room+"\">"+window.location.href+"?room="+room+"</
a>";
};
```

17. This is the function that will be called when our peer sends a file to us; our browser needs to handle such cases. Here, we will take metadata from the received JSON object and show the relevant information to the customer. We will also show the URL to download the file. After the customer clicks on the URL, his/her browser will download it to the chosen location, as shown in the following code:

```
function onFileReceived(name,size,data) {
    var output = [];
```

18. Construct an information item for a file, as follows:

```
    output.push('<li>just reived a new file: <a href=' + data +
'>', name + '</a> ', size, ' bytes', '</li>');
```

19. Put the information line on the page to make it visible for the customers, by using the following code:

```
    document.getElementById('list').innerHTML = '<ul>' + output.
join('') + '</ul>';
    }
```

20. This callback function is called when the user selects the file(s) he wants to send. Here, we gather details of the files, as we did previously, and show the information line for every selected file using the following code:

```
function handleFileSelect(evt) {
    var files = evt.target.files;
    filelist = files;
```

Kindly note that the preceding `filelist` variable is within the global scope. The following part of code will go through the list of files and collect its properties (for example, filename and size) in the `output` array. Then we will show these properties on the HTML page in a user-friendly form.

```
    var output = [];
    for (var i = 0, f; f = files[i]; i++) {
        output.push('<li><strong>', escape(f.name), '</strong> (',
f.type || 'n/a', ') - ', f.size, ' bytes, last modified: ',
f.lastModifiedDate ? f.lastModifiedDate.toLocaleDateString() :
'n/a',
                    '</li>');
    }
    document.getElementById('list').innerHTML = '<ul>' + output.
join('') + '</ul>';
};
</script>

</body>
</html>
```

Running the application

Now we're ready to test our file-sharing application. This can be done by performing the following steps:

1. Go to the project's root folder and compile the signaling server using the following command:

   ```
   rebar clean
   rebar get-deps
   rebar compile
   ```

2. If you're under the Linux box, start the signaling server using the following command:

   ```
   erl -pa deps/*/ebin apps/*/ebin -sasl errlog_type error -s
   rtcserver_app
   ```

3. If you're using the Windows box, use the following command to start the signaling server:

   ```
   erl -pa deps/cowboy/ebin deps/cowlib/ebin deps/gproc/ebin deps/
   jsonerl/ebin deps/ranch/ebin apps/rtcserver/ebin -sasl errlog_type
   error -s rtcserver_app
   ```

4. Now, point your web browser to the domain or IP address where the application is accessible. You should see two buttons and a link (URL). In the following screenshot, you can see Chrome and the main page of the application:

5. Open the link in another web browser or any other computer; you should see a similar page there. I used Firefox as a second peer, as you can see in the following screenshot:

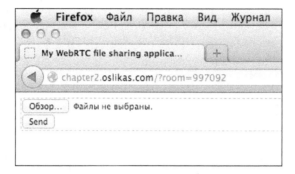

Kindly note the opened link in the address field.

6. Next, click on the **Choose Files** button in the first browser and choose a file you want to send. After you have chosen the file, you should see the detailed information appearing on the page (the name, size, last modified date, and so on). The following screenshot represents this stage:

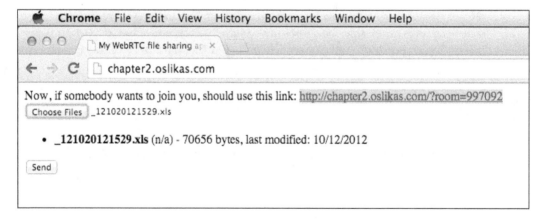

7. Now, click on the **Send** button in the first browser; the file will be transmitted to the remote peer (the second browser; Firefox, in my case).

8. On the second browser, you should see the filename and its size appearing on the page where the URL should also appear, as shown in the following screenshot:

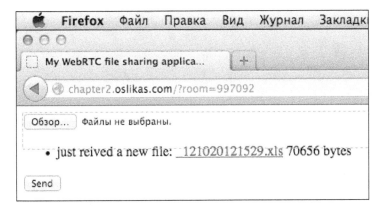

In the screenshot, you can see that Firefox just received the file from Chrome and you can see the appropriate link.

9. Now, you can right-click on the link and select the **Download to...** option; your browser will download the file and then save it to the chosen location.

Summary

We developed a simple peer-to-peer file-sharing application using the WebRTC DataChannel API. Using it, two peers can establish a direct connection between each other and send files to each other. You can choose just one file to transmit or you can select a list of files and they will be transmitted one by one.

You also got a brief practical introduction to the HTML5 File API and learned how to use it to work with the filesystem from JavaScript.

In the next chapter, we will delve deeply into the WebRTC API and develop an application that will be able to stream a prerecorded peer-to-peer video. This application will also be able to share a desktop to the remote peer.

3
The Media Streaming and Screen Casting Services

In the previous chapter, we learned about data channels and developed a simple file-sharing application that uses direct peer-to-peer connections. We learned about data channel types, got introduced to terms such as TLS/DTLS and SRTP/SCTP, and also covered which data channel type is suitable for what kind of tasks.

We also utilized the HTML5 File API functions when working with the file system in the JavaScript code, and we will use this knowledge when developing the demo application in this chapter.

In this chapter, we will use our knowledge about data channels and develop an application that provides two new useful features: streaming prerecorded videos and screen casting (demonstrating a screen to the remote side in real time).

Streaming prerecorded media is a standard feature of the WebRTC technology. It allows peer A to stream the prerecorded media to peer B, who can play it online. How can this be useful in real life? For example, you have your marriage video recorded and you would like to show it to your parents who live in another country, thousands of miles away from you. How can you show the video to your parents? You could use any file-storing service or even a postal service, but it would be time consuming and expensive. Using WebRTC and HTML5, you can set up your private media streaming service in minutes and stream your family video to your parents online.

The following is how Wikipedia describes the feature that we are going to implement during the development of the application:

> *"Streaming media is multimedia that is constantly received by and presented to an end-user while being delivered by a provider. Its verb form, "to stream", refers to the process of delivering media in this manner; the term refers to the delivery method of the medium rather than the medium itself.*
>
> *A client media player can begin playing the data (such as a movie) before the entire file has been transmitted. Distinguishing delivery method from the media distributed applies specifically to telecommunications networks, as most other delivery systems are either inherently streaming (e.g., radio, television) or inherently nonstreaming (e.g., books, video cassettes, audio CDs). For example, in the 1930s, elevator music was among the earliest popularly available streaming media; nowadays Internet television is a common form of streamed media. The term "streaming media" can apply to media other than video and audio such as live closed captioning, ticker tape, and real-time text, which are all considered "streaming text". The term "streaming" was first used in the early 1990s as a better description for video on demand on IP networks; at the time such video was usually referred to as "store and forward video", which was misleading nomenclature."*

Screen casting is mostly an experimental feature, and at the time of writing this, it is supported by Chrome alone. Nevertheless, other browsers are supposed to implement it in the near future. Using the screen casting feature, you can display your screen to the other side using just a web browser; it will be able to see your screen in its browser window. For example, you need to give some kind of assistance to your younger sister (or a grandma) with a website. Before the release of WebRTC, you would have to use some special software to see their desktop and give advice. Now, you can easily set up your own screen casting web service; you just need to open the web page, and you can see your peer's desktop.

The term *screen casting* can be understood in different ways, creating misunderstandings and disappointments. In particular, Wikipedia describes a screencast as follows:

> *"A screencast is a digital recording of computer screen output, also known as a video screen capture, often containing audio narration. The term screencast compares with the related term screenshot, whereas screenshot generates a single picture of a computer screen, a screencast is essentially a movie of the changes over time that a user sees on a computer screen, enhanced with audio narration."*

Nevertheless, don't be confused:

- We will not record the screen, but we will demonstrate it to the remote side in the live mode (we will stream the desktop).

- We will not use the audio in this feature; we will use only the video (we will stream the live-captured desktop screen).

- Using this feature, it is not possible to remotely control the desktop yet, although this feature has a great potential for remote support and any kind of professional, commercial, or e-learning scenarios.

As done earlier, our new application will be built using the server part (the signaling server) and the client-side code will be executed in a web browser (the application itself) using JavaScript. The signaling server will be used only during the stage of establishing a connection; all the data exchange (when streaming prerecorded media or when sharing a desktop) will be implemented using peer-to-peer direct connections. We discussed p2p connections in detail in *Chapter 1, Developing a WebRTC Application*.

We will also delve a bit deeper into using HTML5 and the File API:

- Reading a file from JavaScript code, slicing it into chunks
- Using the `MediaSource` and `SourceBuffer` objects to render the media data

Preparing our environment

The new application that we will develop in this chapter needs some additional environment preparations in order to work:

- An HTTP secure layer (HTTPS)
- A WebSocket proxy
- A configured web browser to enable features
- A WebM media file

Using HTTPS and SSL

Hypertext Transfer Protocol Secure (HTTPS) is a communication protocol that enables secure communications over computer networks. In particular, HTTPS is widely deployed on the Internet. Actually, HTTPS is not even a protocol. HTTPS is the result of simply layering **Hypertext Transfer Protocol** (HTTP) on top of the SSL/TLS protocol. In other words, HTTPS is a result of the encapsulation of the HTTP protocol into SSL/TLS. Thus, HTTPS adds the security capabilities of SSL/TLS to the standard HTTP communications.

You can find more information about HTTPS on Wikipedia at
`http://en.wikipedia.org/wiki/HTTP_Secure`.

Technical details on HTTPS are available in the appropriate RFC at
`http://tools.ietf.org/html/rfc2818`.

Transport Layer Security (**TLS**) uses long-term public and private keys when
exchanging a short-term session key to encrypt the data flow between the client
and the server. Thus, the security of HTTPS is provided by SSL/TLS.

You can learn more about TLS on Wikipedia at `http://en.wikipedia.org/wiki/`
`Transport_Layer_Security`.

You can read more RFCs on TLS at `http://tools.ietf.org/html/rfc5246`.

While establishing a secure connection, there has to be some kind of guarantee that
you are talking to the partner you want to talk to. To achieve this goal when using
HTTPS, X.509 certificates are used. As a consequence, a public key infrastructure and
certificate authorities (**CA**) are necessary in order to verify the relation between the
owner of a certificate and the certificate itself. It is also necessary to have certificate
authorities to generate and sign a certificate as well as administer the validity of
the certificates.

You can find more information about X.509 on Wikipedia at `http://en.wikipedia.`
`org/wiki/X.509`.

Technical details of X.509 are available at `http://www.ietf.org/rfc/rfc2459.txt`.

A detailed explanation on certificate authorities can be found at `http://`
`en.wikipedia.org/wiki/Certificate_authority`.

As we said before, HTTPS is widely used over the Internet, and it provides the
authentication of websites and associated web servers. HTTPS also serves to protect
websites and their users against man-in-the-middle kind of attacks. Additionally, it
provides bidirectional encryption of communications between a client and a server.
In practice, using HTTPS provides a reasonable guarantee that one is communicating
with precisely the website that one is intended to communicate with (as opposed
to an imposter). As a consequence, using HTTPS, we can also be assured that the
contents of the communications between the user and the site cannot be read or
forged by any third party.

Historically, HTTPS was primarily used for payment transactions on the Web as well
as for e-mail and sensitive transactions in corporate information systems. The situation
has changed in the late 2000s and early 2010s when HTTPS began to be widely used to
protect the authenticity of a webpage on all types of websites, securing accounts and
keeping user communications, identities, and web browsing private.

First of all, the application should use HTTPS, and this is something that a web server has to support and have it configured in an appropriate way. So, you need to configure your web server properly. This requirement is mandatory for screen casting; this feature just won't work if you're using HTTP and not HTTPS. Another feature, media streaming, will work well with any protocol, HTTP or HTTPS.

Please refer to your web server documentation to learn how to configure an HTTPS layer properly; we will not touch on this topic in detail here because different web servers have different ways to configure this option.

You can find instructions on how to configure HTTPS for most popular web servers at the following links:

- Apache: `http://httpd.apache.org/docs/current/ssl/ssl_howto.html`
- NGINX: `http://nginx.org/en/docs/http/configuring_https_servers.htm`
- Microsoft IIS: `http://support.microsoft.com/kb/324069`

Please note that you need a valid SSL certificate to configure HTTPS on the web server. There are several companies, such as Verisign and Thawte, that can emit SSL certificates. Usually, you will have to pay some amount of money per year for the certificate. Nevertheless, some companies provide certificates free of cost; for example, StartSSL (`https://www.startssl.com/`).

For testing purposes, you can use a self-signed certificate. You can generate it by yourself. There are also several services on the Web that can help you with this task. For example, `http://www.selfsignedcertificate.com/`.

You can also do it manually, referring to *Chapter 4, Security and Authentication*. We will discuss this topic in more detail and learn how to create self-signed SSL certificates for testing purposes. So, please, generate a valid SSL certificate and configure your web server to use the HTTPS protocol before proceeding.

Configuring a WebSocket proxy

As you know from the previous section, we need to configure our web server to support the HTTPS protocol. I hope you have completed this task successfully and your web server is now secure.

Now, we have to improve another important part of our future application: WebSocket. We use the WebSocket protocol as a transport layer for our signaling mechanism. The problem is that when we use HTTPS and the web browser loads HTML pages from the web server using the secure protocol, the WebSocket connections also have to be established using a secured layer.

If a website uses HTTPS, then all its content has to be completely hosted over HTTPS, and it must not have any content loaded over HTTP; otherwise, the user might be vulnerable to attacks and malware. For example, even if a website does use HTTPS but some JavaScript files are loaded insecurely over HTTP on an HTTPS page, then the user might be vulnerable to attacks.

If a website has a certain web page that contains sensitive data or information (the login page, payment data, user profile, and so on) of the website loaded securely over HTTPS but the rest of the website is loaded insecurely over HTTP, then there is a big chance that the user will be vulnerable to many kinds of attacks. On such a website, the user and the HTTP session will be exposed every time the site is accessed via HTTP instead of HTTPS. Therefore, cookies on a website served over HTTPS need to have the secure attribute enabled.

In other words, the web browser will prohibit an insecure WebSocket connection on an HTML page loaded using HTTPS. So, both the signaling server (which uses WebSocket) and the web server have to be secured and made accessible by HTTPS.

Actually, browsers behave in various ways in such situations; Chrome will open a page using a secure layer and will accept the insecure WebSocket connection; on the other side, Firefox will throw an error message in the console.

Anyway, we want our application to work well and be friendly with the world, so we need to make our signaling mechanism via the WebSocket connection secure too.

We can do this in two ways:

- Make the signaling server work over HTTPS (configure our Erlang server to support SSL certificates and the HTTPS layer)
- Change the client code to create the WebSocket connections not directly to the signaling server but to the web server using HTTPS; then, proxy all WebSocket requests on the web server from clients to the signaling server locally

The first approach is more difficult and complex. We don't want to get deep into the configuration stuff.

The second way is simpler and is the way that I'd suggest you to go with. With this option, we also need to make a little change in the web server's configuration, but these changes are much simpler and involve fewer steps compared to choosing the first option.

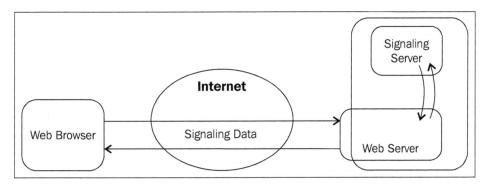

In the preceding figure, you can see how a WebSocket proxy should work:

- A web browser doesn't contact the signaling server directly. The signaling server is not accessible from the Internet and listens on the local network interface only.

- A web browser contacts the web server when establishing a signaling channel. The web server then works as a proxy; it retransmits requests from the web browser to the signaling server and vice versa.

- A signaling server communicates with the web server; it doesn't establish a direct connection with the web browser.

Using this, we support HTTPS for the signaling channel, and we have the signaling server hidden from the web server. The less of the signaling server is seen from the Internet, the better it is.

The following is an example of how to configure the Nginx web server to proxy all the WebSocket requests from the clients to a local server (nginx.conf).

Using `location`, the web server will proxy all the requests committed to the following path from a client (a customer's web browser) to the actual location of our signaling server:

```
location /signaling {
```

The following port is where the signaling server is running. The web server will proxy all the requests performed to the preceding path and route them to the following URL:

```
proxy_pass http://localhost:30000;
```

We need to set up the HTTP protocol version to be used; according to the standard, for WebSocket, it should be `1.1` at least:

```
proxy_http_version 1.1;
```

WebSocket requests are implemented as HTTP upgrade requests. So, we need to let the web server know that we want to work with such headers:

```
proxy_set_header Upgrade $http_upgrade;
proxy_set_header Connection "upgrade";
```

Upgrade the header field of the HTTP protocol that was introduced in Version 1.1. In the exchange between the client and the HTTP server, the client should begin with making a clear-text request to the server. The request will then be either upgraded to a newer version of an HTTP protocol, or switched to a different protocol.

The connection upgrade must be requested from the client side. In case a server wants to enforce an upgrade, it can send a *426 upgrade required* response; in this case, the client should send a new request with the appropriate upgrade headers.

WebSocket uses an upgrade mechanism to establish a connection with an HTTP server using the compatible way. The WebSocket protocol consists of two parts:

- A handshake and establishing the upgrade connection to the server
- Actual data transfer

First of all, a client should request for a WebSocket connection using two headers, *Upgrade: WebSocket* and *Connection: Upgrade*. The request also has to contain a few protocol-specific headers (for example, the HTTP protocol version) in order to set up a handshake.

Then the server, if it supports the protocol, has to reply with same *Upgrade: WebSocket* and *Connection: Upgrade* headers and complete the handshake.

After the handshake stage is completed successfully, the actual data transfer begins.

The following are the less relevant and nonmandatory options, nevertheless, they can be useful; we don't want HTTP redirects, and we ask web server to send the customer's real IP address to the signaling server (otherwise, the signaling server won't know the customer's IP address because the customer will not connect to the signaling server directly but a via web server proxy):

```
proxy_redirect off;
proxy_set_header   Host             $host;
proxy_set_header   X-Real-IP        $remote_addr;
proxy_set_header   X-Forwarded-For  $proxy_add_x_forwarded_for;
}
```

If you're using a web server other than Nginx, please refer to the web server's documentation to find out how to configure the WebSocket proxy functionality. You can find relevant instructions for other popular web servers at the following resources:

- **Apache**: http://httpd.apache.org/docs/2.4/mod/mod_proxy_wstunnel.html
- **Microsoft IIS**: http://blogs.technet.com/b/erezs_iis_blog/archive/2013/09/16/new-features-in-arr-application-request-routing-3-0.aspx

The web browser configuration

By default, Firefox and Chrome have disabled some options that we need to enable in order to make our application work.

For Firefox, open the URL about:config, and you will see a list of browser configuration options. Look for media.mediasource.enabled and set it to true. Otherwise, the prerecorded media streaming won't work.

For Chrome, open the chrome://flags URL and you will see its configuration options. Look for the **Enable screen capture support in getusermedia()** string in the list and click on the **Enable** button. This feature is necessary to make the screen casting feature work in Chrome.

These options are disabled by default because they are (like many other WebRTC features) still under active development. Actually, this is something that is being done on an experimental basis. So, probably after the WebRTC is standardized, your customers won't need to touch these browser options and everything necessary will be enabled by default. However, for now, you have to remember this limitation, and for today, you have to ask your customer to enable these options manually.

Preparing a media file

To test the prerecorded media-streaming feature, we need to prepare the media file that we will stream. For our application, we will use the WebM media files.

You can prepare/encode such video files yourself, or can download them from `http://www.webmfiles.org/demo-files/`.

Of course, you can prepare such media files manually using a simple video editor or a video encoder that is usually supplied with popular operating systems:

- iMovie for Mac OS X
- Movie Maker for MS Windows
- Avidemux for Linux

Just record a video using your webcam (or take an existing video, if you have any), and convert it to the `.webm` format using a standard tool for your operating system.

Developing the application

In this chapter, we're going to develop a new WebRTC application that will implement two different features: media streaming and screen casting.

For the customer, these two features seem to be something different and not related to each other. Nevertheless, they both use a very similar code base and WebRTC API mechanisms. Thus, we will implement both these features in one application.

In other words, using the application we're going to develop in this chapter, the customer will be able to utilize either the screen casting function, or the prerecorded media streaming; moreover, these features can work in parallel.

Developing a signaling server

There are still no major changes in the signaling server that we developed in the first chapter, so we can use it here for the new application.

The only change that we need to implement in the application that was developed in *Chapter 1, Developing a WebRTC Application*, is related to HTTPS and the proxy that we just discussed. We need to change the path where the server will accept requests from clients.

Edit the `www/apps/rtc_server/src/rtcserver_app.erl` file.

Find the following piece of code there:

```
Dispatch = cowboy_router:compile([
                        {'_',[
                            {"/", handler_websocket,[]}
                        ]}
                    ]),
{ok, _} = cowboy:start_http(websocket, 100, [{port, 30000}], [
```

Change the preceding code to the following one:

```
Dispatch = cowboy_router:compile([
                        {'_',[
                        {"/signaling", handler_websocket,[]}
                            ]}
                    ]),
{ok, _} =
cowboy:start_http(websocket, 100, [{port, 30000} ,{ip,{127,0,0,1}}],[
```

As you can see, we changed the path where the server will wait for requests. Also, we asked it to bind to the local network interface on the IP address 127.0.0.1 (localhost).

Limitations

The screen casting feature is an experimental feature, and for now, only Chrome can stream the desktop. Other browsers (for example, Firefox) can receive the screen cast data streamed by Chrome and show it, but they don't support screen casting itself as yet.

Streaming of prerecorded media can work differently in different browsers:

- Firefox will start playing the streamed data right after it has received the first chunk
- Chrome will wait until all the chunks are received (the whole media file) and will start playing only after that

The media streaming and screen casting service

We are finished with the server side (the signaling server) and web server configurations; now it's time to write some code in JavaScript.

Our application will have two features: prerecorded media streaming and screen casting.

For the first feature, we will read the media file chunk by chunk and send its binary data to the remote side using the WebRTC data channels we learned about in the previous chapter. The remote side will receive these chunks and play back the media in real time.

The second feature is experimental, and currently, only Chrome can screen cast the desktop; we will use a special media type for this, and a lot of code will be very similar to the code we learned in *Chapter 1, Developing a WebRTC Application*.

Developing a WebRTC API wrapper

We will use our API wrapper to make the development process easy and convenient.

In general, the wrapper will be very similar to the one we developed for the first two chapters. Some code will be taken from *Chapter 1, Developing a WebRTC Application*, and some code will be borrowed from *Chapter 2, Using the WebRTC Data API*.

I suggest you to not spend much time on reused code pieces introduced in previous chapters and discuss new code only. So let's start!

Edit the www/myrtclib.js file:

```
var RTCPeerConnection = null;
var webrtcDetectedBrowser = null;

var getUserMedia = null;
var attachMediaStream = null;
var reattachMediaStream = null;
```

We declare two variables for the local and remote streams. The screen casting picture will be transmitted using standard media streams (such as the video in the first chapter):

```
var localStream;
var remoteStream;
```

Nevertheless, we declare only the remoteVideo control because we want to see the remote desktop, but it makes no sense to display the local one:

```
var remoteVideo;
```

When streaming media between peers, we will read the local filename and send it to the remote peer in little pieces, one by one. The `chunkSize` variable declares the size of such a piece to be transmitted. You can play with bigger values. In general, it depends on the network; for a local network with low latency, you can set a bigger value; for the Internet, it makes sense to set a lower value. Here, we use `1200` bytes per chunk; this could be good for the Internet:

```
var chunkSize = 1200;

var room = null;
var initiator;

var pc = null;
var signalingURL;
```

Here, we declare two variables for the data channels, but actually, we will use only one data channel (like in the previous chapter). Here, we need two variables to make the process of the establishment more convenient:

```
var sendDChannel = null;
var recvDChannel = null;

var channelReady;
var channel;
```

The following is a control variable to handle the HTML5 video element that we will use to display the remote desktop:

```
var videoScreen;

var pc_constraints = {"optional": [{RtpDataChannels: true}]};
var data_constraint = {reliable :false};

var pc_config = {"iceServers":
    [{url:'stun:23.21.150.121'},
     {url:'stun:stun.l.google.com:19302'}]};
```

For the media streaming feature, we will read the media files piece by piece and transfer them to the remote peer. On the remote-side peer, we will receive such pieces (chunks), put them into a memory buffer, decode them, and play them using the video HTML5 tag.

The following variable is a variable that will point to such a buffer:

```
var receiverBuffer = null;
```

When the remote peer is streaming the media, we need to show it to the user. As we discussed previously, we will receive little chunks from the remote peer one by one and put them into a memory buffer. We need this buffer to be connected to a media source entity, and this entity should be linked to the HTML5 video tag; then, we will ask the browser to render and display the receiving media content.

So, we need the following variable to control the media source entity:

```
var recvMediaSource = null;
```

The following initialization function is very similar to functions that we developed in the previous chapters. Here, we initialize the control variables and open a connection to the signaling server:

```
function myrtclibinit(sURL, rv) {
    signalingURL = sURL;
    initWebRTCAdapter();
    if (webrtcDetectedBrowser === 'firefox' ||
(webrtcDetectedBrowser === 'chrome' && webrtcDetectedVersion >= 31)) {
        pc_constraints = null;
        data_constraint = null;
    }

    remoteVideo = rv;

    openChannel();
};
```

The following function will establish a new connection to the signaling server. In this application, we don't have the web chat feature (like the one we have in the application in *Chapter 1, Developing a WebRTC Application*), and the signaling server is used to establish a direct peer-to-peer connection:

```
function openChannel() {
    channelReady = false;
    channel = new WebSocket(signalingURL);
    channel.onopen = onChannelOpened;
    channel.onmessage = onChannelMessage;
    channel.onclose = onChannelClosed;
};
```

When a signaling channel is opened, we create a direct peer-to-peer connection, decide whether we are the caller or we're waiting for the call, and get access to the browser's media:

```
function onChannelOpened() {
    channelReady = true;
    createPeerConnection();

    if(location.search.substring(1,5) == "room") {
        room = location.search.substring(6);
        sendMessage({"type" : "ENTERROOM", "value" : room * 1});
        initiator = true;
    } else {
        sendMessage({"type" : "GETROOM", "value" : ""});
        initiator = false;
    }
    doGetUserMedia();
};
```

The following functions are called when we get a message from the signaling server and when the signaling channel has been closed for some reason:

```
function onChannelMessage(message) {
    processSignalingMessage(message.data);
};

function onChannelClosed() {
    channelReady = false;
};
```

The following function is used to send a message to the signaling server and to process back the messages received from it:

```
function sendMessage(message) {
    var msgString = JSON.stringify(message);
    channel.send(msgString);
};

function processSignalingMessage(message) {
    var msg = JSON.parse(message);
```

```
        if (msg.type === 'offer') {
            pc.setRemoteDescription(new RTCSessionDescription(msg));
            doAnswer();
        } else if (msg.type === 'answer') {
            pc.setRemoteDescription(new RTCSessionDescription(msg));
        } else if (msg.type === 'candidate') {
            var candidate = new RTCIceCandidate({sdpMLineIndex:msg.
label, candidate:msg.candidate});
            pc.addIceCandidate(candidate);
        } else if (msg.type === 'GETROOM') {
            room = msg.value;
            OnRoomReceived(room);
        } else if (msg.type === 'WRONGROOM') {
            window.location.href = "/";
        }
    };
```

The following function is called when we get access to the browser's media. Code is very similar to what we used in *Chapter 1, Developing a WebRTC Application*. The difference is that here, we want to get access to the screen but not the video camera; notice the `chromeMediaSource` keyword.

Also, please pay attention to the fact that we need to set the `audio` option to `false`, and this is important. Otherwise, our application won't be provided with access to the browser's media.

This probably a temporary limitation and will be changed in the future:

```
function doGetUserMedia() {
    var constraints = {"audio": false, "video": {"mandatory":
{chromeMediaSource: 'screen'}, "optional": []}};
    try {
        getUserMedia(constraints, onUserMediaSuccess,
            function(e) {
                console.log("getUserMedia error "+ e.toString());
            });
    } catch (e) {
        console.log(e.toString());
    }
};
```

The following function is called when we get access to the browser's media. Here, we store the local media stream and add it to the peer connection created previously:

```
function onUserMediaSuccess(stream) {
    localStream = stream;
```

```
            pc.addStream(localStream);

            if (initiator) doCall();
    };
```

This is how we create a peer-to-peer connection:

```
    function createPeerConnection() {
        try {
```

Please note that we create a peer connection, and we also create a data channel:

```
            pc = new RTCPeerConnection(pc_config, pc_constraints);
            pc.onicecandidate = onIceCandidate;
            pc.ondatachannel = recvChannelCallback;
            pc.onaddstream = onRemoteStreamAdded;
        } catch (e) {
            console.log(e);
            pc = null;
            return;
        }
    };
```

The following function is called when the remote peer has added its media stream to the peer connection; here, we get the stream and link it to the HTML5 `video` tag:

```
    function onRemoteStreamAdded(event) {
        attachMediaStream(remoteVideo, event.stream);
        remoteStream = event.stream;
    };
```

We want to a create data channel like we did in the previous chapter, while developing a file-sharing application. A data channel will be used to transmit the prerecorded media data to the remote side:

```
    function createDataChannel(role) {
        try {
            sendDChannel = pc.createDataChannel("datachannel_"+room+ro
    le, data_constraint);
        } catch (e) {
            console.log('error creating data channel ' + e);
            return;
        }
```

We will track the channel's state and log it for debugging, so here are the two listeners:

```
sendDChannel.onopen = onSendChannelStateChange;
sendDChannel.onclose = onSendChannelStateChange;
}
```

The function we used in all our applications in the previous chapters helps us establish peer-to-peer connections via firewalls and NAT:

```
function onIceCandidate(event) {
    if (event.candidate)
        sendMessage({type: 'candidate', label: event.candidate.
sdpMLineIndex, id: event.candidate.sdpMid,
            candidate: event.candidate.candidate});
};
```

The callback functions are called when we use the WebRTC API functions and fail. Pay attention as these callback functions are mandatory; for example, your application won't get access to the browser's media if you omit this callback, executing the getUserMedia function:

```
function failureCallback(e) {
    console.log("failure callback "+ e.message);
}
```

The following function is called when we want to make a call to the remote side. The function right next to it is called when we get a call and want to answer it. This code is similar to one we used in the previous chapters:

```
function doCall() {
    createDataChannel("caller");
    pc.createOffer(setLocalAndSendMessage, failureCallback,
errorCallBack);
};

function doAnswer() {
    pc.createAnswer(setLocalAndSendMessage, failureCallback,
errorCallBack);
};

function errorCallBack(e) {
    console.log("Something is wrong: " + e.toString());
};
```

The following are functions that are already known to operate with SDP and communicate to the signaling server:

```
function setLocalAndSendMessage(sessionDescription) {
    pc.setLocalDescription(sessionDescription);
    sendMessage(sessionDescription);
};

function sendDataMessage(data) {
    sendDChannel.send(data);
};
```

The following function is called when we get a data channel opened successfully. Here, we report that the channel is opened, and we set an event listener to receive messages from the remote side via this data channel:

```
function onSendChannelStateChange() {
console.log('Send channel state is: ' + sendDChannel.readyState);
if (sendDChannel.readyState === 'open') sendDChannel.onmessage =
onReceiveMessageCallback;
}
```

The following callback function is executed when the remote side opens a data channel to us. Here, we want to store the new channel ID and set the event listeners to work with the channel:

```
function recvChannelCallback(evt) {
    console.log('Receive Channel Callback');
    recvDChannel = evt.channel;
    recvDChannel.onmessage = onReceiveMessageCallback;
    recvDChannel.onopen = onReceiveChannelStateChange;
    recvDChannel.onclose = onReceiveChannelStateChange;
}
```

The following function is the event listener for a data channel state change:

```
function onReceiveChannelStateChange() {
console.log('Receive channel state is: ' + recvDChannel.readyState);
```

As we discussed in the beginning of the chapter, we use the sendDChannel and recvDChannel variables to handle the data channel between peers. When we make a call, we use the first one, and when we need to answer, we use the second one. Technically, we use *one* channel, *not two* channels; so in the following code, we make these two variables equal to the same channel ID:

```
if (recvDChannel.readyState === 'open') sendDChannel = recvDChannel;
}
```

The following function is called when we get a message from the remote side via a data channel. As with the signaling server, we use a JSON object to exchange messages between peers:

```
function onReceiveMessageCallback(event) {
    try {
        var msg = JSON.parse(event.data);
```

To indicate to the remote side that we want to start the streaming, we use the `streaming_proposed` type of message. If some of the peers receive such a message, it means that the peer needs to get ready to start receiving the media data and play it back:

```
if (msg.type === 'streaming_proposed') {
    doReceiveStreaming();
}
```

We will send the media data by chunks in messages of type `chunk`. If a peer gets such a message, it should extract the media data from the received message and render it by playing it back:

```
        else if (msg.type === 'chunk') {
            onChunk(msg.data);
        }
    }
    catch (e) {}
};
```

The following function is called when we want to start streaming the media file to the remote side. It takes the filename as an input:

```
function doStreamMedia(fileName) {
```

Send the `streaming_proposed` message to the remote side via the data channel. This indicates that the remote side has to get ready, and we will start transmitting the media in seconds:

```
var msg = JSON.stringify({"type" : "streaming_proposed"});
sendDataMessage(msg);
```

To read the media file, we will use the HTML5 File API; we touched on this topic in the previous chapter while learning about file sharing.

For file reading operations, we will use the `FileReader` entity introduced by the modern HTML5 File API:

```
var fileReader = new window.FileReader();
```

An event listener is called when we get read access to the file:

```
fileReader.onload = function (e) {
    startStreaming(new window.Blob([new window.Uint8Array(e.
target.result)])));
};
```

The following code will load the media file into an array of bytes:

```
fileReader.readAsArrayBuffer(fileName);
```

We need to send the media file to the remote peer part-by-part. Here, we loaded the entire file into a buffer, and now we will slice it into parts (chunks) and send them one-by-one:

```
function startStreaming(blob) {
    if(!blob) return;
```

We have the file size and we will start sending it from the beginning, moving ahead block by block:

```
var size = blob.size;
var startIndex = 0;
var addition = chunkSize;
```

The following function actually does the work. It takes a part of a media file and sends it to the remote peer:

```
function netStreamer() {
```

We need another `fileReader` entity because we want to slice the media file into equal blocks (chunks) and read them one by one:

```
fileReader = new window.FileReader();
```

The following function is the callback function that is called when we read a block from the media file:

```
fileReader.onload = function (e) {
```

The following code gets the next chunk and creates an array of bytes on it:

```
var chunk = new window.Uint8Array(e.target.result);
```

Send the block to the remote peer. Here, we're sending a piece of media file to the remote peer using the established data channel connection:

```
pushChunk(chunk);
```

Add the block size to the index to read the next block at the next time:

```
startIndex += addition;
```

If we still have a block in the file, call the function again; it will read and send the next block of data. Here, we use some a trick of calling the `requestAnimationFrame` function to avoid freezing the browser's UI:

```
if (startIndex <= size) window.requestAnimationFrame(netStreamer);
```

If the block is the last one, we send a message to the remote side, mentioning that this is the end and we will not transmit any additional media data for now:

```
        else pushChunk({end: true});
    };
```

Read the file by slices. Actually, here we have a BLOB object where the file exists as binary data, and we just ask `fileReader` to slice this BLOB and call our preceding callback function:

```
            fileReader.readAsArrayBuffer(blob.slice(startIndex,
    startIndex + addition));
        }
```

At the following point, we start the actual streaming process:

```
        netStreamer();
    }
};
```

We call this function when we get the `streaming_proposed` message from the peer and want to show the streaming media to the user:

```
function doReceiveStreaming() {
```

First of all, we need to create the `MediaSource` object:

```
    recvMediaSource = new MediaSource();
```

Here we declare the event listener function that will be called when the `MediaSource` object has been created successfully:

```
    recvMediaSource.addEventListener('sourceopen', function (e) {
```

In this function, we create a media buffer and connect it to the MediaSource object. This is the buffer into which we will put the received chunks of media.

As you can see, we set the media type and codec we want to use. This information is important for the browser in order for it to know how to render the received media data and how to show it to the user.

In real life, we should parse the chosen file, detect the metadata, and send it to the remote peer before sending any actual media data to it.

Nevertheless, here we will hardcode this data because working with media files and detecting the media type in JavaScript can be a vast topic; therefore it is written as a separate chapter:

```
        receiverBuffer = recvMediaSource.addSourceBuffer('video/
webm; codecs="vorbis,vp8"');
            console.log('media source state: ', this.readyState);
        }, false);
```

We also call the event listener when we are done reading the media data. Nothing critical here; we use it just for debugging purposes. Nevertheless, such a function can be used to create any actions automatically when the streaming is over:

```
    recvMediaSource.addEventListener('sourceended', function (e) {
            console.log('media source state: ', this.readyState);
        }, false);
```

This is how all this magic stuff is connected to the visible world. Here, we link the `MediaSource` object to the HTML5 video object that we use to show the streaming media to the user:

```
    videoScreen.src = window.URL.createObjectURL(recvMediaSource);
        };
```

This function is executed when we get a new media chunk for the remote peer. We construct an array of bytes from it and put it into the media buffer. The web browser will do the rest of the work automatically:

```
    function doAppendStreamingData(data) {
        var uint8array = new window.Uint8Array(data);
        receiverBuffer.appendBuffer(uint8array);
```

If the video object is paused, ask it to start playing the receiving media. Otherwise, the streaming process might continue but video won't be shown:

```
        if (videoScreen.paused) videoScreen.play();
    };
```

We received a note that mentioned that the streaming is over and no media data will be sent; so convey this to the `MediaSource` object:

```
    function doEndStreamingData() {
        recvMediaSource.endOfStream();
    };
```

We use this function to send chunks to the remote side. Here, we construct the chunk message, put the binary data into it, and send it using the data channel:

```
function pushChunk(data) {
    var msg = JSON.stringify({"type" : "chunk", "data" : Array.
apply(null, data)});
    sendDataMessage(msg);
};
```

The following callback function is executed every time we get the chunk message from the remote peer. It takes the data as binary chunks, extracted from the message. Here, we check here whether the stream is over yet or not and pass the data to another function that will put it into the media buffer:

```
function onChunk(data) {
    if (data.end) doEndStreamingData();
    else doAppendStreamingData(new Uint8Array(data));
};
```

Creating the application's index page

We finished with the JavaScript code, and now we can write some HTML to visualize all the magic.

Edit the www/index.html file:

```
<!DOCTYPE html>
<html>
<head>
    <title>My WebRTC media streaming and screen casting
application</title>
```

We want our UI to look good, so let's start with the CSS style definitions. With the following CSS section, we describe two entities, for a video element and for a container:

```
<style type="text/css">
    video {
        width: 384px;
        height: 288px;
        border: 1px solid black;
        text-align: center;
    }
    .container {
        width: 780px;
        margin: 0 auto;
```

```
        }
    </style>
    <script type="text/javascript" src="myrtclib.js"></script>
    <script type="text/javascript" src="myrtcadapter.js"></script>
</head>
<body onLoad="onPageLoad();">
<div class="container">
```

The following HTML video tag will be used later to display the remote desktop when using our screen casting feature:

```
    <video id="videoscreen" autoplay controls></video>
```

The following element will be used to display the prerecorded content transmitted from the remote side to the user:

```
    <video id="remotevideo" autoplay></video>
</div>
<div class="container">
```

The following `div` element is called `status` and will be used later to display the link for another side in order to connect to our virtual room:

```
    <div id='status'></div>
```

Using the file selection control, the customer can choose a media file that it would like to stream to the remote side. Remember that for this application, we support only WebM media files. This is not a limitation of WebRTC, but we would implement more complex logic in order to support a bigger list of media files, and it definitely is out of the scope of this book:

```
    <div><br>
        ...then select .webm file you want to stream <input
type="file" id="files" name="files[]"/>
    </div>
```

The following code configures the button that the customer needs to click on to start the streaming. After the button is clicked on, the streaming process will begin. We will read the selected media file slice by slice and send it to the remote peer. The remote peer will receive these slices, render them, and show them to the user using its `video` element:

```
    <div>
        ...and then press <button onclick="onSendBtnClick()">Start
streaming !</button>
    </div>
</div>
```

Again, we can't implement all the functionality using just HTML (even using modern HTML5), and we need some help from good old JavaScript:

```
<script>
```

The following is the variable where we will get the file name that the user has chosen:

```
var filelist;
```

Let's do some preparations before we can begin the magic. The following function will be called exactly after the web page has been loaded. Here, we need to perform some preliminary steps:

```
function onPageLoad() {
```

Take control over the video element. We will use this element to display the remote desktop when screen casting:

```
videoScreen = document.getElementById("videoscreen");
```

We use the HTML5 API because web browsers are too old and do not support it. We need to check whether this API is accessible in the browser we're working under and display an alert in case it isn't. Otherwise, we will get an unhandled error (exception):

```
    if (window.File && window.FileReader && window.FileList && window.
Blob) {
    } else {
        alert('The File APIs are not fully supported in this
browser.');
        return;
    }
```

The following callback function will be executed when the user has chosen a media file. We have to react to this to get the media file name and prepare for the next actions:

```
    document.getElementById('files').addEventListener('change',
handleFileSelect, false);
```

Initialize the WebRTC API. Please note that we use a secure WebSocket connection here, `wss://`, but not `ws://`, which we used in the previous chapters. It is important to use a secured WebSocket connection on the page, loaded via HTTPS; we discussed this question in detail at the beginning of the chapter:

```
    myrtclibinit("wss://<YOUR_DOMAIN>/signaling", document.
getElementById("remotevideo"));
    };
```

The following function is called when the user pushes the **Start streaming!** button. We take the filename and pass it to the `doStreamMedia` function discussed earlier; it will start reading the file by slices and streaming them to the remote peer:

```
function onSendBtnClick() {
    doStreamMedia(filelist[0]);
};
```

The callback function is called from our API wrapper that was developed earlier. It is called when we registered ourselves on the signaling server and got the virtual room number. We construct a URL that should be opened on a remote side to establish a direct connection:

```
function OnRoomReceived(room) {
    var st = document.getElementById("status");
    st.innerHTML = "Now, open this link on other browser window or
machine: <a href=\""+window.location.href+"?room="+room+"\">"+window.
location.href+"?room="+room+"</a>";
};
```

A simple event listener is called when the user chooses a file. Here, we get control over the file list element. We store the pointer to the file list entity and will use it later to control it (for example, get the selected file name):

```
function handleFileSelect(evt) {
    filelist = evt.target.files;
};
</script> </body> </html>
```

Starting the application and testing it

Now it's time to test our application:

1. Compile and start the signaling server as described in one of the previous chapters.

2. Open your application's URL in a web browser. Let's open the URL in Chrome.

3. You might see a message on Chrome that says **Do you want <website name> to share your screen?** Click on **YES** here, and you will see the "sharing screen" plaque at the bottom of the screen. At this stage, your application gets access to the screen and is ready to show it to the remote side.

4. You will also see a URL on the page that you should open on the remote side. Copy this URL and open it in another browser or another machine. Let's open it in Firefox. Firefox won't ask you whether you want to share the screen; it doesn't support this feature yet, so it will stream the video from your camera instead of the screen.

5. After the peer connection has been established successfully, you should be able to see the remote desktop in Firefox and the video from the camera in Chrome.

6. Now, in Chrome, select a WebM media file and click on **Start streaming**. The transmission should start immediately and Firefox should start playing back the media received from Chrome.

7. The vice versa streaming (from Firefox to Chrome) will also work, but Chrome might wait until it receives all the media data and start playing it back only after that. Such behavior seems to be a temporary limitation due to the technical issue, and we can only hope that it will be fixed in one of the next versions of Chrome.

8. Please note that you have to explicitly point your web browser to use secure layer protocol (HTTPS) when navigating to the application main page.

Summary

We developed a great application that demonstrates two features of the WebRTC technology: screen casting and pre-recorded media streaming.

The media streaming feature is still under active development and is not supported by WebRTC API natively, so we used our skills and knowledge obtained in the previous chapters to implement this functionality using Data Channels.

The second feature, screen casting, is not natively supported by most web browsers. Actually, for now, it is supported only by Chrome, and it is a very raw experimental feature. Nevertheless, we implemented this functionality in our application.

Please note that both the features are under development, and there is no standard way to make it compatible with all the web browsers. Thus, you should probably improve the code after the features are standardized.

We obtained additional useful knowledge on configuring the necessary infrastructure: the WebSocket proxy and HTTPS layer on the web server.

In the next chapter, we will delve deep into security questions, learn how to deploy and configure the TURN server, and integrate it into our application. We will also configure the authorization mechanism in the TURN server and develop a new application that will be able to use this feature.

We will discuss why you might want to use STUN or TURN in some cases and what the difference in scope of security is.

We will learn how to create SSL certificates for our applications and how to use them for the TURN security.

We will also cover why STUN is always a public resource and why it is dangerous for the TURN server to be public.

4
Security and Authentication

In the previous chapter, we learned how to deal with the HTML5 File API to read files from a JavaScript application. We obtained knowledge on how to work with the media streaming the WebRTC API.

We also developed an application based on our newly acquired knowledge, which provides two useful features: screen casting and streaming of prerecorded media. Using the first feature, a customer can show their screen to a remote peer. Using the second feature, a customer can stream a prerecorded media file directly to a remote peer without any upload/download file operations. Both features just work in a web browser.

While developing our application, we also acquired basic knowledge on HTTPS and its configuration at the web server's side. We found out why it is important to use a secure layer and why it is highly recommended that you use it (some of the WebRTC features might work incorrectly or won't even work at all if you don't use a secure layer).

In this chapter, we will learn more on security and authentication in the scope of developing WebRTC applications. In particular, we will learn the following topics:

- **Using STUN and TURN servers**: We discussed a bit about this topic in *Chapter 1, Developing a WebRTC Application*. Now, since we have additional experience, we will talk on this in detail.

- **Using TURN authentication**: Here, we will talk on why authentication is necessary for TURN. We will also learn how to utilize this feature in our application.

- **Using web-based identity providers and Single Sign-On (SSO)**: These are the features of the WebRTC API.

- **Configuring HTTPS and emitting certificates**: In *Chapter 3, The Media Streaming and Screen Casting Services,* we acquired basic knowledge on HTTPS. Now, we will discuss this in more detail.

- **Configuring your own TURN server with authentication**: With our knowledge of topics such as TURN/STUN technologies and HTTPS/SSL, we will learn how to install and configure our own TURN-server-supported authentication; also, we will develop an application integrated with this server.

In this chapter, we will develop a simple application that will use authentication to utilize our TURN server.

We will also learn how to create self-signed SSL certificates and use them in our application and TURN server.

Preparing our environment

In general, WebRTC is a cross-platform technology that enables you to build cross-platform applications. Nevertheless, you might need to use additional services or technologies that may be platform dependent; the configuration process of such services can also be different for different platforms.

For example, in this chapter we will need to compile and configure the TURN server, and this process might be very different for Linux and Windows (especially the compiling process). In this chapter, we will learn topics by assuming that we're using a Linux/BSD-based environment. So, you need a Linux box with standard developer tools installed (for example, gcc/cc, make, or autotools).

You also need an OpenSSL package to be installed – it will be necessary to create self-signed certificates.

To install all the necessary packages, please use your system's default package manager tool. For example, for Ubuntu, it is apt-get or aptitude tools.

Signaling

According to the WebRTC standard, all of its components have to support and use encryption. Nevertheless, the standard doesn't describe the signaling mechanism. As you know from *Chapter 1*, *Developing a WebRTC Application*, you can use any protocol to provide the signaling mechanism for your application. It can even be an electronic mail or a snail mail. So, there is no standard that would describe the signaling mechanism and protocols for a WebRTC application. Thus, there is no standard that would describe security-related questions in the scope of signaling. Therefore, signaling has to be secure (this is mandatory), but it is totally up to you to make it secure.

In this book, we use WebSocket as a transport for the signaling mechanism in our applications. WebSocket is not a secure protocol by itself. To make it secure, we performed the following additional steps:

1. Configured HTTPS on the web server.
2. Configured the WebSocket proxy on the web server.
3. Made the signaling server listen on the local network interface only (localhost).
4. Established a connection with our signaling server using `wss://`, asking the web browser to use a secured WebSocket connection (over HTTPS).

You can refer to *Chapter 3*, *The Media Streaming and Screen Casting Services*, for more details.

The bottom line is whichever signaling mechanism you use should be secure.

Using STUN and TURN

As you know from *Chapter 1*, *Developing a WebRTC Application*, WebRTC uses the ICE technology and utilizes STUN/TURN servers when establishing a peer-to-peer connection process to break through firewalls and NAT. The difference between using STUN and TURN is schematically visualized in the following diagrams (we also used these diagrams in *Chapter 1*, *Developing a WebRTC Application*):

The following diagrams show a peer-to-peer connection using the STUN server:

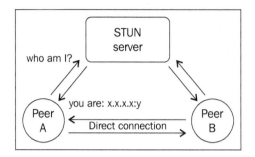

The following diagram represents a general simple case of when the TURN server is used. Here, we have a situation where both peers use the same TURN server. We can see that peers use the STUN server to discover their network parameters and use the TURN server exchanging with media data. Technically, every TURN server can also serve as a STUN server. So, in the diagram, the STUN and TURN servers are represented as separate entities, but in the real world, they are usually one physical TURN/STUN server.

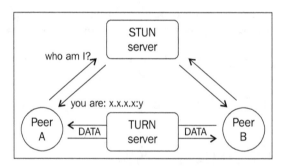

On the other hand, when you use the TURN server, all data and media are not exchanged directly between the peers, but via the TURN server. This means that all the traffic that is exchanged by the peers is transmitted via the TURN server. So, you can't just switch it off after a peer-to-peer connection has been established; otherwise, the connection will be dropped.

In the first chapter, we also learned how to configure a simple STUN server and use it in our application, but we have not touched the part about configuring the TURN server yet because this topic is a bit more complicated than installing a STUN server. Now, we will go deeper into TURN configuration in the scope of security and authentication.

As you can see in the previous diagrams, in the case of the STUN server, it will be used only during the connection establishing process. After the peer connection has been established, all data and media will be exchanged between the peers directly; at this stage, the STUN server can even be shut down, as it doesn't affect the peers anymore.

You might ask, why then do we need to use TURN? Why can't we use just STUN? Why do we need to route all peers' traffic via the TURN server that does not use a direct connection?

The answer is pretty simple. In most cases, it would be enough to use STUN, but for many clients, this technology doesn't work (usually because of very strict firewalls). In such kinds of cases, you can try to use TURN (for most clients, it will solve this situation).

Approximately, we can say that STUN works for around 76 percent of cases, and for 24 percent of cases, it will fail and peer-to-peer connection won't be established. For these 24 percent of cases, you can use TURN and it will work for around 80 percent of these.

You can pass STUN servers as far as TURN servers to the ICE framework when creating the RTCPeerConnection object (described in *Chapter 1, Developing a WebRTC Application*). In this case, the web browser will try to establish a direct connection between the peers using STUN servers. For the transport layer (the protocol peers will exchange their data with this layer), it will try to use the UDP protocol by default. If it fails, the browser will try to use the TCP protocol. Moreover, if this idea also fails, the browser will start trying to use any of the passed TURN servers. Again, first it will try to use UDP as a transport layer and then use TCP in case UDP fails. Thus, the order in which the STUN/TURN servers' list passed to the ICE framework doesn't matter.

Usually, TURN servers can also act as STUN. So, you don't need to configure STUN and TURN servers separately — but, of course, it is possible.

Using the TURN authentication

From *Chapter 1, Developing a WebRTC Application*, you know that we used such a construction to get a new peer connection object:

```
var pc = RTCPeerConnection(pc_config, pc_constraints);
```

The pc_config parameter in the preceding code is a set of configuration options that we want to use while creating the peer connection object.

In the previous chapter, we used only the STUN technology, and usually, `pc_config` was something similar to the following:

```
var pc_config = {"iceServers":
        [{url:'stun:23.21.150.121'},
         {url:'stun:stun.l.google.com:19302'}]};
```

Here, you can see the two URLs of the ICE servers (we also discussed the ICE framework in *Chapter 1, Developing a WebRTC Application*), and they are both STUN servers.

In the same way, we can refer to a TURN server as follows:

```
{
  'iceServers': [
    {
      'url': 'stun:stun.l.google.com:19302'
    },
    {
      'url': 'turn:turn1.myserver.com:12345?transport=udp',
      'credential': 'UGJKBJHVYT',
      'username': '3214234:32324234'
    },
    {
      'url': 'turn:turn2.myserver.com:12346?transport=tcp',
      'credential': 'HKJUHBHG',
      'username': '23249:98437'
    }
  ]
}
```

Here, you can see that we added two more servers and they're TURN servers. Pay attention as we're also passing the following additional parameters to each TURN server:

- username: Basically, this is a login or the username entity that the web browser should use to pass authorization to the server.

- credential: This is just the password entity used to pass the authorization.

- ?transport: This is not a separate option in the pc_config object but a part of each URL. Note that we use the udp value for the first TURN server, and we use tcp for the second one. By passing this parameter, we can ask the web browser to use a desirable transport layer while working over the TURN server — TCP or UDP.

As you just found out, we need to know the credentials (login/password) in order to work with TURN servers. On the other side, STUN servers don't need such kind of information. Moreover, STUN servers don't even support authorization.

In other words, your STUN server will be freely accessible to anyone on the Internet. Anyone will be able to use it for their own needs, as far as you can freely use any STUN server you've found on the Internet. The bottom line is *any STUN server technically is a public resource*. Basically, this is why we used Google's public STUN servers to develop our WebRTC applications in the previous chapters.

It might sound weird and dangerous. Why is there no mechanism to make the STUN server private? The answer is simple: because there is actually nothing dangerous or incorrect to have the STUN server as a public resource. The only work that the STUN server does is exchange some data in order to help two peers to establish a direct peer-to-peer connection. It consumes very low amounts of network traffic and other resources, and such a kind of service (STUN) is very specific; also, the STUN session is very low cost and lives for a limited amount of time. So, basically, it just doesn't make any sense to make STUN a private resource that needs authorization.

On the other side, let's take a look at the TURN server. As you can see in the second diagram at the beginning of the chapter, in the case of TURN technology, all the traffic between the peers goes through the TURN server. This means that peers don't exchange data directly; peer A sends its data (a binary stream of audio/video, other media, or whichever sort of data they're exchanging) to the TURN server, and then the TURN server sends (retransmits) the received data from peer A to the remote peer B; and vice versa.

Here we see a totally different situation: if someone uses our TURN server, it will route all its traffic via the server. Who do you think will pay for this traffic and the other consumed resources? Of course, the server's owner!

This is why you can find a public STUN server, but you actually won't find any official public TURN server. No one wants to pay for someone's traffic. Also, just imagine how big the amount of media traffic might be: for example, Skype can consume around 700 MB per hour for one continuous video-audio call. Of course, it depends on the video/audio quality; the better the quality, the larger the amount of traffic.

Therefore, TURN servers do support authentication. Moreover, production TURN servers usually don't support nonauthenticated access like STUN servers do (nevertheless, TURN servers technically can serve without authentication, as well). So, while using TURN servers in your application, you have to pass a username/password for every TURN server that you use.

The TURN transport layer

As we discussed previously, we can pass the nonmandatory parameter ?transport for every TURN server in its URL; we also learned that this parameter can be equal to udp or tcp. By default, if this parameter is not passed, the UDP protocol will be used as a transport layer. If it fails, the TCP protocol will be used.

Usually, it is fine (probably better) to use UDP because of the following reasons:

- It is more lightweight than TCP
- No sent/received confirmations, and because of this, less latency
- In case of network problems, some media frames will be dropped (usually, it is better than trying to retransmit them and get the network stuck)

Nevertheless, you can use TCP if you need it (for example, if you definitely know that the UDP protocol is prohibited by a firewall policy on a peer).

The TURN REST API

This API is a draft yet and the original description document is available at http://tools.ietf.org/html/draft-uberti-rtcweb-turn-rest.

The main aim of this API is to provide some mechanism that can enable dynamic temporary passwords, which can be used with TURN servers while authenticating.

The general schema of such a TURN authentication mechanism is as follows:

- The client (the web browser) sends a request to the server (a server-side application) asking for TURN credentials. Optionally, the request can also include the username.
- The server responds with the TURN URL, username, and password.
- The client uses these credentials to authenticate with the TURN server.

Kindly note that the credentials are temporary (time limited).

The response from the server will be as follows:

- **Username**: This is the TURN username that the client has to use while authenticating. This name is a colon-delimited combination of the expiration timestamp and the username parameter from the client's original request. If the username is not specified, the server can use any other value here.

- **Password**: This is the TURN password that the client has to use when authenticating. This value is calculated by the server using an algorithm like `base64(hmac(secret key, username))`. The TURN server and the server application both share the same secret key. So, the TURN server will do the same calculations and will compare them with the credentials received from the client.

- **TTL**: This value represents the time to live parameter. It is optional, and we won't use this field in our application.

- **URIs**: This field represents an array of URLs of the available TURN server(s). In our case, we will send just one URL to our own TURN server.

Detailed explanations can be found in the original draft by using the link at the beginning of this section.

Using web-based identity providers

The WebRTC API has some methods to provide the web-based identity and **SSO** (**Single Sign-On**) mechanism.

As you know from *Chapter 1, Developing a WebRTC Application*, there are two entities in the scope of a peer-to-peer connection establishing mechanism: offer and answer. Both of these entities can be authenticated by using the web-based identity providers as far as the channels are established using the RTCPeerConnection method.

The key idea is that the side that sends the offer/answer also acts as the **Authenticating Party** (**AP**) and obtains an identity assertion from the **IdP** (**identity provider**) which then attaches it to the offer/answer entity. Next, the remote peer (the consumer of the offer/answer entity) acts as the **Relying Party** (**RP**) and verifies the assertion. Such magic with the IdP is designed to decouple the web browser from any particular identity provider. The web browser should only know how to load the IdP's JavaScript (which is dependent on the IdP's identity) and the generic protocol to request and verify assertions.

The IdP should provide the necessary logic to bridge the generic protocol to the IdP's specific requirements. Thus, a web browser can support any number of identity protocols.

The generic protocol details are described in the WebRTC security architecture at `http://datatracker.ietf.org/doc/draft-ietf-rtcweb-security-arch/`. This document specifies and describes the procedures required to instantiate the IdP proxy, requests identity assertions, and consumes the results. For now, this mechanism is still not implemented in the WebRTC API.

Deploying the TURN server

In *Chapter 1, Developing a WebRTC Application,* we discussed how to install, configure, and deploy a simple STUN server for our needs. Here, we will deal with the TURN server, which can also act as a STUN server. So, you don't need to have both the servers (but you can); you can configure just one and it will work either as a STUN or TURN server.

There are several TURN server implementations on the Internet, and you can take what you like the most, but I'd recommend that you consider the `rfc5766-turn-server` project for use in production systems.

You can download the source codes from `https://code.google.com/p/rfc5766-turn-server/`.

You need to install additional packages before compiling the server, in particular, `mysqlclient-dev`, `libevent`, `libmysqlclient-dev`, `libevent-dev`, and `libssl-dev`. Kindly note that the package list may vary for different Linux distributions.

Unpack the source code into a folder and run the following command line:

```
./configure
```

This will prepare the product for compilation and will show you the errors or a list of the necessary additional packages, if any. This is a usual way to compile programs under Linux, so if you have any experience with this, everything we're talking about here shouldn't be new for you.

Next, we need to compile it and install it on the system, so run the following command in the command line:

```
make
```

This will perform the compilation. If you don't see any errors, execute the following command:

```
make install
```

The last command is not mandatory. It will install the product on your system. By default, it uses the `/usr/local` prefix (for most systems). If you execute this command, you can find the product executable file under the prefix `bin` folder. Otherwise, it will be left under the folder in which you compiled it, so you can execute it from there.

Configuring HTTPS and self-signed certificates

As we discussed, it is very important to use encryption and security for WebRTC. In *Chapter 3*, *The Media Streaming and Screen Casting Services*, we learned how to use HTTPS and SSL certificates in general. From the same chapter, you already know that some of the WebRTC features won't even work if you're not using secure layers.

So, your application definitely needs an SSL certificate. For production systems, you will need to use SSL certificates emitted by trusted centers, such as Verisign, Thawte, or others. You can also start with `http://startssl.com`.

For testing purposes, you can use your own self-signed SSL certificates. It is easy, free of charge, and a quick way to start. But there are some limitations, and self-signed certificates are not acceptable for use on production systems. Though the certificate implements full encryption, your website visitors will see the f ollowing browser warning:

The certificate should not be trusted!

To create self-signed certificates, you need an OpenSSL package installed on your system. This can be done by performing the following steps:

1. Generate a private key. It's time to go to the command line and enter the following commands:

   ```
   $ openssl genrsa -des3 -passout pass:x -out server.pass.key 2048
   $ openssl rsa -passin pass:x -in server.pass.key -out server.key
   ```

   On running the preceding commands, the following output will be generated:

   ```
   writing RSA key
   $rm server.pass.key
   ```

2. Generate a certificate-signing request by using the following command. When it prompts you for a password, just press return.

   ```
   $ openssl req -new -key server.key -out server.csr
   ...
   Country Name (2 letter code) [AU]:US
   State or Province Name (full name) [Some-State]:California
   ...
   A challenge password []:
   ...
   ```

3. Generate an SSL certificate by using the following command:

```
$ openssl x509 -req -days 365 -in server.csr -signkey server.key
-out server.crt
```

4. Copy the certificates to the appropriate configuration folder of the TURN server by using the following command:

```
cp server.crt /usr/local/etc/turn_server_cert.pem
```

```
cp server.key /usr/local/etc/turn_server_pkey.pem
```

Now this certificate can be used with your web server and the TURN server (we will discuss this further in this chapter).

Configuring the server's firewall

TURN (as far as STUN) uses the TCP/UDP ports to work. So, if your server has a firewall (I'm pretty sure it has) configured, you need to be sure that the following TURN server's ports are accessible from the Internet (connections allowed from any port to any port):

- 3478 TCP
- 3478 UDP
- 5349 TCP
- 5349 UDP

You can find more details on firewalls on Wikipedia at http://en.wikipedia.org/wiki/Firewall_(computing).

On Linux boxes, usually, the iptables tool is used to configure and control the system's firewall.

To make your TURN server work properly, you also should have a public IP address that can be used by the server.

Configuring the TURN server

The configuration file of the TURN server can be found at /usr/local/etc/turnserver.conf.

There are many options and parameters in the configuration file, but we will discuss only the necessary ones. The configuration file is itself well documented. The default TURN listener port for UDP and TCP is 3478, as we discussed previously. To improve security, you can use different ports. Don't forget to set it explicitly in your application when creating the RTCPeerConnection object, as shown in the following code:

```
listening-port=3478
```

The following is the TURN listener port for TLS. As we learned, we should use as much secured mechanisms as possible. So, it is definitely a good idea to configure our own TURN server to use secure ports and encryption.

```
tls-listening-port=5349
```

The nonencrypted TCP/UDP sessions can connect to the TLS/DTLS port. Also, the encrypted TCP/UDP sessions can connect to the nonencrypted port by default; this is allowed by the configuration: the TURN server can recognize the type of traffic. For secured TCP connections, this TURN server implementation currently supports SSL Version 3 and TLS versions 1.0, 1.1, and 1.2. For secured UDP connections, it supports DTLS Version 1.

The next option is an alternative listening port for UDP and TCP listeners. You can set up an alternative port, and it can be useful in some cases. For example, you can configure your TURN server to listen on standard ports, but some clients/peers can have firewalls that block such ports. In such a case, it might be useful to configure additional (alternative) ports for the TURN server to listen on. It does not necessarily solve the problem, but it might help.

If you use alternative ports, you can pass them as a separate TURN server(s) while creating the RTCPeerConnection object. By default, this value is set to zero and it means the listening port plus one.

```
alt-listening-port=0
```

The same parameter for an encrypted session can be configured as follows:

```
alt-tls-listening-port=0
```

In the listener IP address of the relay server, you should explicitly specify an IP address (or IP addresses) of the TURN server. Otherwise, it will use all of the existing IP addresses of the machine. This is not something bad actually, but usually you would want to know exactly which resources are in use.

```
listening-ip=x.x.x.x
listening-ip=y.y.y.y
```

The relay address is the local IP address that will be used to relay the packets to the peer.

This is what the documentation says on this option:

> "*The same IP(s) can be used as both listening IP(s) and relay IP(s). If no relay IP(s) are specified, then the TURN server will apply the default policy: it will decide itself which relay addresses to be used, and it will always be using the client socket IP address as the relay IP address of the TURN session (if the requested relay address family is the same as the family of the client socket).*"

So, basically, in most cases you don't want to use this option and will change the default behavior.

```
relay-ip=x.x.x.x
```

The default values of the lower and upper bounds of the UDP relay endpoints are set to 49152 and 65535, respectively. These are the ports that the TURN server will use for relay. In most cases, you won't want to change these values. Nevertheless, if you're developing an application (and deploying the TURN server) for some specific circumstances and you definitely know that some specific set of ports are prohibited by a firewall, this option might be useful. These values are set as follows:

```
min-port=49152
max-port=65535
```

The next options are not actually directly related to security; they're related to debugging. Nevertheless, they can be very useful during the development process, so let's take a look at them. The verbose option, if uncommented, will switch the server to the verbose mode. I suggest you use the verbose mode the first time, because the server will show more useful information then. The #Verbose option, if uncommented, will switch the server to the *extra verbose* mode. The TURN server documentation says that this mode is very annoying and produces lots of output. It also says that using it is not recommended under any normal circumstances. So, don't forget to turn it off when you finish debugging.

By uncommenting the following option, we're switching on the long-term credential mechanism:

```
lt-cred-mech
```

For our current purposes, the short-term credential mechanism option should be switched off (commented out). Nevertheless, for your other applications, you may prefer to use this option rather than the preceding one. For more details, please refer to the documentation on TURN server implementation. The following is the short-term credential mechanism option:

```
#st-cred-mech
```

The following option is opposite to `lt-cred-mech` and `st-cred-mech`. The TURN server with the no-auth option enabled allows anonymous access. This can be very useful for debugging, but don't leave this option enabled on the production server!

```
#no-auth
```

The TURN REST API flag

The TURN REST API flag is the flag that sets a special authorization option based on the authentication secret. This feature can be used with the long-term authentication mechanism only (remember what we just discussed).

This feature's purpose is to support the TURN Server REST API—this is a draft of a standard on a REST API for access to TURN services, and you can find it at `http://tools.ietf.org/html/draft-uberti-rtcweb-turn-rest`.

From the documentation:

> *"This allows TURN credentials to be accounted for a specific user ID. If you don't have a suitable ID, the timestamp alone can be used. This option is just turning on secret-based authentication. The actual value of the secret is defined either by the static-auth-secret option, or can be found in the turn_secret table in the database."*

In our case, we need this option to be switched on; we will use the functionality in our application as follows:

`use-auth-secret`

Static authentication secret value (a string) is for the TURN REST API only.

The following option will contain a secret key that we will use in our application to construct TURN username and password. This secret key should be known to the TURN server and to the application—they both should share the same secret key.

In production systems, you have to change this secret key from time to time (usually, once a day would be enough). Here we will use a static value just to demonstrate how this mechanism works, as shown in the following code:

```
static-auth-secret=abc
```

We will not store authentication data (the secret value for secret-based, timed authentication using the TURN REST API) in a MySQL database. We have decided to use a static option as you can see in previous item. Nevertheless, for production systems, you should not use a static value and should use some kind of database to store the secret key and share it between the application and the TURN server. The following option assumes you use MySQL for this and describes a connection string for a MySQL user database. For our application we don't use it, so it is commented out. I left it here just to let you know where you can find it.

```
# mysql-userdb="host=<host> dbname=<database-name> user=<database-user>
password=<database-user-password> port=<port> connect_timeout=<seconds>"
realm=mycompany.org
```

The per-user allocation quota (number of parallel sessions) by default is 0 (no quota, unlimited number of sessions per user). The TURN server allows you to limit your users by the number of sessions it can use in parallel. Again, this is not directly related to security. Nevertheless, it can be a security problem — if you don't control your resources and your customers can consume as much resources as possible.

Usually, this depends on your service. For example, for low-plan customers, you can set 1 session per user; for VIP users, you can set it to zero (no limits).

For now, let's set it to 3, as shown in the following code:

```
user-quota=3
```

The total allocation quota is the total amount of sessions your TURN server will service in parallel. This value depends on the amount of traffic you can pay for and on the amount of users your service can service in parallel, as well as many other factors.

In general, it is a bad idea to leave it as zero, but the specific service will have the specific value here. For our application, let's set a limit, as shown in the following code:

```
total-quota=10
```

The per-session bandwidth quota is in bytes. By default, the value is 0 (no quota, unlimited traffic per session). The following option limits every session with some amount of bandwidth. Pay attention to every session and not to every peer. It means that if you have the user-quota value equal to 3 (as in the preceding code), you have 3 possible sessions for each customer in parallel. And to understand how much bandwidth every customer will get, you need to multiply this value to the following option's value. In production you will probably want to set up some specific value here, but for simplifying we will leave it as it is (no limit), as shown in the following code:

```
#max-bps=0
```

The following two options if uncommented will disable plain (unencrypted) UDP and TCP listeners of the TURN server. For testing purposes, you can keep them enabled, but on the production system you can disable both.

```
no-udp
no-tcp
```

Similar options are present for encrypted listeners (TLS and DTLS). Remember — we want to use as much secured components as possible, so the following options should be commented out on the production system, but for testing purposes and debugging you can enable them.

```
#no-tls
#no-dtls
```

The `nonce` option is directly related to security, as given in the following documcnetation:

"Uncomment if extra security is desired, with nonce value having limited lifetime (600 secs). By default, the nonce value is unique for a session, but it has unlimited lifetime. With this option, the nonce lifetime is limited to 600 seconds, after that the client will get a 438 error and will have to re-authenticate itself."

In our application, we don't plan to use this extra security, so we will leave it commented out (disabled). Although, for your other applications you might want to use it.

```
#stale-nonce
```

The following options are related directly to SSL and certificates, which we will discuss in this chapter. They're necessary, and without them, TLS/DTLS connections won't work.

Note that it might be reasonable to comment out these options and to not use encryption for the first time until you have TURN working and properly integrated with your application. It might be easier to debug it while using non-encrypted TURN running with `verbose` mode enabled.

The following `.pem` files are those we generated in this chapter before. For the certificate file, use an absolute path or a path relative to the configuration file as follows:

```
cert=/usr/local/etc/turn_server_cert.pem
```

For a private key file, use an absolute path or a path relative to the configuration file. Use the PEM file format, as shown in the following code:

```
pkey=/usr/local/etc/turn_server_pkey.pem
```

Private key file password, if it is in encoded format. For our purposes, we use a key without a password. If you use this, you have to specify it in the following option:

```
#pkey-pwd=
```

As you know, the TURN server can also act as a STUN server. The following two options allow you to suppress one of these functionality. You can make it just a TURN or just a STUN server. By default, it will support both TURN and STUN technologies.

For our purposes, we will leave both options commented out. For debugging purposes you can change them.

```
#stun-only
#no-stun
```

The following option describes the username/timestamp separator symbol (character) in the TURN REST API. As you may remember, we use this functionality in our application for the authentication feature.

```
rest-api-separator=:
```

This is the flag that can be used to disallow peers on the loopback addresses (`127.x.x.x` and `::1`). This is an extra security measure, but I'd suggest using it.

Again, for testing and debugging purposes you can use loopback clients, and in that case, you should comment out these options to allow such kind of functionality.

```
no-loopback-peers
```

This is the flag that can be used to disallow peers on well-known broadcast addresses (224.0.0.0 and above and FFXX:*). This is an extra security measure. In general, this is really an extra measure, but it can be useful to enable it in order to prevent network attacks on your service.

```
no-multicast-peers
```

This is an option to set the maximum time, in seconds, allowed for full allocation establishment. Default is 60 seconds. It is the time limit (timeout) during which a new connection should be fully established. You should use here some short values in order to prevent a DOS attack on your service (in particular, your TURN server). The server will drop connection if it has not been fully established during this time limit.

```
max-allocate-timeout=30
```

The following option enables you to allow or ban specific IP addresses or ranges of IP addresses:

> *"If an IP address is specified as both allowed and denied, the IP address is considered to be allowed. This is useful when you wish to ban a range of IP addresses, except for a few specific IPs within that range.*
>
> *This can be used when you do not want users of the TURN server to be able to access machines reachable by the TURN server, but would otherwise be unreachable from the Internet (for example, when the TURN server is sitting behind a NAT)."*

For our purposes, we can leave it as it is. For now, we don't use this functionality, but you can use it for your other projects.

```
# Examples:
# denied-peer-ip=83.166.64.0-83.166.95.255
# allowed-peer-ip=83.166.68.45
```

Mobility with ICE (MICE) specs support.

> *"While moving between networks, an endpoint has to change its IP address. This change breaks upper layer protocols such as TCP and RTP. Various techniques exist to prevent this breakage, all tied to make the endpoint's IP address static (for example, Mobile IP, Proxy Mobile IP, and LISP). Other techniques exist which make the upper layer protocol ambivalent to IP address changes (for example, SCTP). The mechanisms described in this document are in that last category."*

You can find more details on the standard's draft at:

```
http://tools.ietf.org/html/draft-wing-mmusic-ice-mobility
```

For our purposes, we don't use this functionality, so leave this option commented out, as shown in the following code:

```
#mobility
```

We need a username to run the process. After the initialization, the TURN server process will make an attempt to change the current user ID to that user.

To be more secure, it is highly recommended to not run services under root privileges. So, here you should specify the username you created before, especially for your TURN server.

```
proc-user=<user-name>
```

We also need a group name to run the process. After the initialization, the TURN server process will make an attempt to change the current group ID to that group.

You should also specify a separate group for the TURN server, as shown in the following code:

```
proc-group=<group-name>
```

The local system IP address needs to be used for the CLI server endpoint. The default value is 127.0.0.1.

This is the IP address and port for the TURN server console. It can be accessible on them using a password. It is highly recommended to use the default value 127.0.0.1 (local IP). Nevertheless, you can use here an IP address that is accessible from the Internet—in that case, you have to configure your firewall in an appropriate way, as shown in the following code:

```
cli-ip=127.0.0.1
cli-port=5766
```

The default **CLI (console administrator's interface)** access password is empty (no password). You can set a password for it, as shown in the following code:

```
cli-password=<you-cli-password>
```

Do not allow an SSL/TLS version of the protocol. The following are the options that can be used for testing and debugging purposes. In our case, we leave them are commented out.

```
#no-sslv2
#no-sslv3
#no-tlsv1
#no-tlsv1_1
#no-tlsv1_2
```

Integrating the TURN server with our application

Now let's integrate a WebRTC application with our just-deployed TURN server utilizing the authentication mechanism.

We will not introduce any additional specific WebRTC features in this chapter except the one with the TURN authentication, so it doesn't make sense to develop the demo application from scratch. So, we will take the application from *Chapter 1, Developing a WebRTC Application* and improve it.

Thus, in this chapter, I will not provide the complete source codes of the application. We will learn only the new functions and codes that are different from the original application we developed in the first chapter. Please take the application from *Chapter 1, Developing a WebRTC Application*, as the base or refer to the source codes supplied with the book to get the complete code of the application.

As you know from the previous sections, we will generate temporary credentials to authenticate with our TURN server. We also don't want to share this API with everyone; we want to limit the access to our customers only. So, we will allow restricted access to our web application—only registered users will be able to login in and get TURN credentials.

In the following sections, we will learn and comment on only the "improved" parts of the original application and not explain the application's code step by step.

Improving the signaling server

First, we need to calculate the temporary TURN credentials on the signaling server and send them to the web browser. Then, the web browser will use them while connecting to the TURN server.

Open the following web socket handler source code file:

```
apps/rtcserver/src/handler_websocket.erl
```

The following instruction defines the secret key. It should be exactly the same as what we used while configuring our TURN server in the previous section.

Remember that the TURN server and the WebRTC server application both should share the same secret key. The secret key is defined as follows:

```
-define(SECRET_KEY, <<"abc">>).
```

After this, we need to define the TURN URL that will be sent to the web browser. Put either the IP address here that you used while configuring the TURN server in the previous section, or your domain name mapped to this IP address.

Kindly note that we used port 3478; it should also be the same as the one we used while configuring the TURN server in the previous section. Also, note that we explicitly set the UDP protocol to use when working via TURN as follows:

```
-define(TURN_SERVER, <<"turn:YOUR_DOMAIN_OR_IP:3478?transport=udp">>).
```

The following code of the handler has been quoted "as is" to make the logic clear. Only the parts that are commented and explained have been changed.

For a detailed explanation of the rest of the code, please refer to *Chapter 1, Developing a WebRTC Application*.

```
websocket_handle({text,Data}, Req, State) ->
    StateNew = case (State#state.state) of
                  started ->
                      State#state{state = running};
                  _ ->
                      State
              end,
    JSON = jsonerl:decode(Data),
    {M,Type} = element(1,JSON),
    case M of
        <<"type">> ->
            case Type of
                <<"GETROOM">> ->
                    Room = generate_room(),
```

The following code is an improvement. Here, we generate TURN credentials: URL, username, and password. These credentials will be sent to the browser and it will use them when authenticating on the TURN server. The `get_turn_creds` function is defined further in the code as follows:

```
{Turn_URL,Turn_User,Turn_pass} = get_turn_
creds(self()),
```

The following code has been changed as well. In the original code, we generate a new virtual room and send just the GETROOM message back to the web client with the room number attached. Now, we will also generate TURN credentials using the preceding code and send them altogether with the room number to the client.

```
        R = iolist_to_binary(jsonerl:encode({{type, <<"GETROOM">>},
{value, Room}, Turn_URL, Turn_User, Turn_pass})),

            gproc:reg({p,1, Room}),
            S = (StateNew#state{room = Room}),
            {reply, {text, <<R/binary>>}, Req, S, hibernate};
        <<"ENTERROOM">> ->
            {<<"value">>,Room} = element(2,JSON),
            Participants = gproc:lookup_pids({p,1,Room}),
            case length(Participants) of
                1 ->
                    gproc:reg({p,1, Room}),
```

Originally, when we receive the ENTERROOM message from the web browser, it means that someone wants to join the existing virtual room. In that case, we did not send any message to the client. Now we need to generate the appropriate TURN credentials for the client and send them back to it. In the preceding code, we did it for the client that creates a new virtual room; in the following code, we will do the same for a client who joins the existing virtual room.

So, the following code generates TURN credentials:

```
            {Turn_URL,Turn_User,Turn_pass} = get_turn_
    creds(self()),

                        S = (StateNew#state{room = Room}),
```

Also, the following code sends the GETROOM message as well as the packet TURN credentials back to the client:

```
        R = iolist_to_binary(jsonerl:encode({{type, <<"GETROOM">>},
    Turn_URL, Turn_User, Turn_pass}))),
                    {reply, {text, <<R/binary>>}, Req, S, hibernate};
```

The rest of the code is not changed from the original; you can find a detailed explanation of this in *Chapter 1, Developing a WebRTC Application.*

```
            _ ->
                R = iolist_to_
    binary(jsonerl:encode({{type, <<"WRONGROOM">>}})),
            {reply, {text, <<R/binary>>}, Req, StateNew, hibernate}
                end;
        _ ->
                reply2peer(Data, StateNew#state.room),
                {ok, Req, StateNew, hibernate}
            end;
    _ ->
            reply2peer(Data, State#state.room),
            {ok, Req, StateNew, hibernate}
    end;
```

The following function is introduced in this chapter and is absent in the original code. It calculates the TURN credentials that we will send to the web browser (to the client). These credentials will then be used by the client when authenticating on our TURN server that we configured in the previous sections.

```
get_turn_creds(P) ->
```

In the preceding code, when we call the `get_turn_creds` function, we pass the process ID to it. The following code converts the PID from its type to a binary type (the Erlang entity type); we need this conversion further in order to operate with the PID.

```
U = list_to_binary(pid_to_list(P)),
```

The following construction calculates the UNIX timestamp. Yes, Erlang does it in such a nice way.

```
{M, S, _} = now(),
Timestamp = list_to_binary(integer_to_list(M * 1000000 + S + 60)),
```

Then, we need to construct a temporary username. We will do this by concatenating the timestamp and the PID with `:` as a delimiter. So, we will get something similar to `122242324:<1,2,3>`, where `122242324` is the timestamp and `<1,2,3>` is the process ID.

```
Turn_user = <<Timestamp/binary,":",U/binary>>,
```

The following construction calculates the TURN password. The following are the actions that we do here:

- Calculating the HMAC of the TURN username with a static secret key (`abc`) using SHA1
- Encoding the result with base64 as shown in the following code:
  ```
  Turn_pass = base64:encode(crypto:sha_mac(<<"abc">>, Turn_user)),
  ```

The following construction will return TURN credentials and the TURN URL (predefined at the beginning of the module). These TURN details will be sent to the client, and they will use them while authenticating to the TURN server.

```
{{url, ?TURN_SERVER},{username, Turn_user},{credential, Turn_pass}}.
```

Next, we will make the following changes in the main signaling server application module:

- Move HTML and JavaScript files from the `web` project folder into `apps/rtcserver/priv`. We need to do this because we want to implement the restricted access functionality.
- Make the signaling server listen on an external network interface.
- Implement the HTTP web session mechanism.

Open and edit the `apps/rtcserver/src/rtcserver_app.erl` file as shown in the following code:

```
start(_StartType, _StartArgs) ->
    Dispatch = cowboy_router:compile([
                                  {'_', [
```

The following instructions define several URLs that we will serve to the clients: signaling, sign in (here customers can enter their usernames and passwords and get into the restricted area of our application), sign out (using this URL, the client can sign out of our application), conference (here all our HTML and JavaScript codes will be available), and index page (it will represent just a web form with the username and password fields).

```
                        {"/signaling", handler_websocket,[]},
                        {"/signin", handler_signin,[]},
                        {"/signout", handler_signout,[]},
                     {"/conference/[...]", cowboy_static,
{priv_dir, rtcserver, "",[{mimetypes, cow_mimetypes, all}]}},
                        {"/", handler_index,[]} ]} ]),
```

Using the following code, we ask the signaling server to start listening on the external network interface on a TCP port, `21000`; our web application will be available here.

```
{ok, _} = cowboy:start_http(websocket, 100, [{port, 21000}], [
                            {env, [{dispatch, Dispatch}]},
                            {max_keepalive, 50},
                            {timeout, 500},
```

The following construction defines that every request from a client should be processed by the `handler_session` module before it is processed by its own handler. This is necessary to implement the restricted access feature and session mechanism.

```
{onrequest, fun handler_session:on_request/1} ]),

    handler_session:init(),
    rtcserver_sup:start_link().
```

The following section describes the `handler_session` module which implements the HTTP session mechanism – we need to support the restricted access to our application. We learned such modules in the previous chapters, so now we will learn new stuff only.

Open and edit the `apps/rtcserver/src/handler_session.erl` file as shown in the following code:

```
-module(handler_session).
-export([on_request/1, set_session/2, drop_session/1, init/0]).

-include("records.hrl").
```

The following defines the HTTP field name that we will use to operate with sessions:

```
-define(SESSION_NAME, <<"sid">>).
```

Time To Live for session (TTL) is 1 day. If your user has logged in, the session will live for 24 hours, and during this time, the user doesn't need to enter the password again.

```
-define(TTL, 60 * 60 * 24).
```

Create a new ETS table to store sessions. To store known sessions, we will use ETS tables. It is something like a simple in-memory key/value store in Erlang.

```
init() -> ets:new(ets_sessions, [set, named_table, public,
{keypos,1}]).
```

The following function executes for every HTTP request, checks whether the request has a cookie with a session ID, and then routes it to the appropriate URL. In other words, if someone tries to access our restricted area without providing a password, they will be routed to the login page and access will be prohibited until the client provides the correct credentials.

```
on_request(Req) ->
```

We can get cookies from the HTTP header as follows:

```
    {Path, Req1} = cowboy_req:path(Req),
    {SESSID, Req2} = cowboy_req:cookie(?SESSION_NAME, Req1),
```

We can check if we have a session ID there as follows:

```
    case SESSID of
        undefined ->
```

If there is no session, route to the login page as follows:

```
            session_no(Req2, Path);
        _ ->
```

We have a session ID in the HTTP header. Let's check if we have the same session ID in our table on the server.

```
        PEER = load_session(SESSID),
        case PEER of
            undefined -> session_no(Req2, Path);
            _ -> session_yes(Req2, Path)
        end
    end.
```

The following function is called when the user's browser doesn't provide a session ID or the provided session ID is unknown:

```
session_no(Req, Path) ->
```

If the client wants to reach the /conference URL, we will redirect it to the index page with the login form. This URL is available for registered customers only.

```
        case lists:member(Path, [<<"/conference">>]) of
            true ->
        Req1 = cowboy_req:set_resp_header(<<"Location">>, <<"/">>, Req),
                {ok, Req2} = cowboy_req:reply(302, [], "", Req1),
                Req2;
```

If the client wants to reach any other URL, we accept what is shown in the following code:

```
            _ -> Req
        end.
```

The following code is executed when the user's browser provides a session ID and we have such session IDs stored in our database:

```
session_yes(Req, Path) ->
```

If the client wants to reach the signin page or the main page, we will redirect it to the conference. We do this because at this stage we know that the customer is authorized already, so it doesn't make sense to make them sign in again and we can redirect the customer directly to the conference creating area.

```
        case lists:member(Path, [<<"/signin">>, <<"/">>]) of
            true ->
                Req1 = cowboy_req:set_resp_header(<<"Location">>,<<"/
conference">>,Req),
                {ok, Req2} = cowboy_req:reply(302, [], "", Req1),
                Req2;
            _ -> Req
        end.
```

The following function stores the session ID in the user's browser cookie. It is called after the user has successfully signed in.

```
set_session(Req, Data) ->
    SID = generate_session(),
    {M,S,_} = now(),
    T = M * 1000000 + S,
    TTL = T + ?TTL,
    Data1 = Data#session{expires = TTL},
    ets:insert(ets_sessions, {SID, Data1}),
    Req1 = cowboy_req:set_resp_cookie(?SESSION_NAME, SID,
[{path,<<"/">>}] ,Req),
    Req1.
```

We also need some code which would remove the session ID from cookies to implement the sign-out mechanism. The following code does exactly what we want. It is called from the sign-out page.

```
drop_session(Req) -> cowboy_req:set_resp_header(<<"Set-
Cookie">>,<<?SESSION_NAME/binary,"=deleted; expires=Thu, 01-Jan-1970
00:00:01 GMT; path=/">>, Req).
```

The following code looks for the session ID stored locally in ETS. If a session exists but has expired, it removes the session ID from the ETS table and returns an undefined value (no session).

```
load_session(SID) ->
    case ets:lookup(ets_sessions, SID) of
        [] -> undefined;
        [{SID, DATA}] -> DATA
    end.
```

We need some function that will generate the session ID. The following function does this:

```
-spec generate_session() -> binary().
generate_session() ->
    Now = {_, _, Micro} = now(),
    Nowish = calendar:now_to_universal_time(Now),
    Nowsecs = calendar:datetime_to_gregorian_seconds(Nowish),
Then=calendar:datetime_to_gregorian_seconds({{1970,1,1},{0,0,0}}),
Prefix=io_lib:format("~14.16.0b", [(Nowsecs-Then)*1000000+Micro]),
    list_to_binary(Prefix ++ to_hex(crypto:rand_bytes(9))).
```

The following are the set of helper functions used in the preceding function to generate session IDs:

```erlang
-spec to_hex([]) -> [];
            (binary()) -> list();
            (list()) -> list().
to_hex([]) ->
    [];
to_hex(Bin) when is_binary(Bin) ->
    to_hex(binary_to_list(Bin));
to_hex([H|T]) ->
    [to_digit(H div 16), to_digit(H rem 16) | to_hex(T)].

-spec to_digit(number()) -> number().
to_digit(N) when N < 10 -> $0 + N;
to_digit(N) -> $a + N-10.
```

Now we need to implement the index handler – the code that will server index page (/ URL). It will also implement the sign-in mechanism. Open and edit the following file:

apps/rtcserver/src/handler_index.erl

We will edit the file as follows:

```erlang
-module(handler_index).
-export([init/3, handle/2, terminate/3]).
-include("records.hrl").

init({_Any, http}, Req, []) ->
    {ok, Req, undefined}.

handle(Req, State) ->
    {Method, Req1} = cowboy_req:method(Req),
    HasBody = cowboy_req:has_body(Req1),
    {ok, Req2} = process_request(Method, HasBody, Req1),
    {ok, Req2, State}.
```

Here, we process POST requests from the client. This is an attempt to sign in. We will extract the username and password fields from the received web form. Then, we will validate them and decide if we want the user to be legitimate to access our restricted resource area or not.

```
process_request(<<"POST">>, true, Req) ->
    {ok, PostVals, Req1} = cowboy_req:body_qs(Req),
```

Extract email and password from HTTP headers.

```
    Email = proplists:get_value(<<"n_email">>, PostVals),
    Password = proplists:get_value(<<"n_password">>, PostVals),
```

Validate extracted values and perform appropriate action.

```
    V = validate_login(Email, Password),
    case V of
        false ->
            Req2 = Req1,
```

If the credentials are incorrect, the "sign-in failed" page is displayed, as shown in the following code:

```
            {ok, Content} = signin_failed_dtl:render([]),
            cowboy_req:reply(200, [], Content, Req2);
        ID ->
```

If the credentials are OK, we redirect the customer to our restricted resource area, the /conference page, as shown in the following code:

```
            Req2 = handler_session:set_session(Req,#session{id = ID,
    email = Email}),
            {ok, Content} = signin_success_dtl:render([ID]),
            cowboy_req:reply(200, [], Content, Req2)
    end;
```

The following part of the module serves the GET requests. These requests are usual requests from a web browser; we just need to return the index page back to the client.

```
process_request(<<"GET">>, false, Req) ->
    {ok, Content} = index_dtl:render([]),
    cowboy_req:reply(200, [], Content, Req).

terminate(_Reason, _Req, _State) ->
    ok.
```

The following function performs user credential validation. In production, you will use a database, of course. Here, we used the predefined static username and passwords for our demo application.

```
validate_login(Email,Password) ->
  case Email of
    <<"user@myserver.com">> ->
      case Password of
        <<"secretword">> ->
          true;
        _ ->
          false
      end;
    _ -> false
end.
```

Improving the JavaScript browser-side code

We also need to add some code to our JavaScript client code in order to enable the web browser handling of the TURN credentials and implement the authentication feature.

Thus, we need to edit the `apps/rtcserver/priv/myrtclib.js` file by performing the following steps:

1. First, let's take a look at the onChannelOpened function. As you know from the previous chapters, this function is called when the signaling channel is opened.

2. In the original code of the first chapter, we also called the doGetUserMedia function at the end of onChannelOpened. Thus, after the signaling channel is opened, we get access to the media devices, and after that, the magic begins.

3. Now, we need to change this behavior. We can't establish peer connection until we have TURN credentials. So, in the onChannelOpened function, we remove the call of doGetUserMedia. We will call it later after we receive credentials for the TURN server, as follows:

```
function onChannelOpened() {
    channelReady = true;

    if(location.search.substring(1,5) == "room") {
        initiator = true;
        room = location.search.substring(6);
        sendMessage({"type" : "ENTERROOM", "value" : room *
1});
```

```
        } else {
            initiator = false;
            sendMessage({"type" : "GETROOM", "value" : ""});
        }
// kindly note, in the original code we called doGetUser media
here
// now this call should be removed!
    };
```

4. The next function we have to change is the following one. This function is also present in all our applications that we developed in the previous chapters. This function parses and processes messages from the signaling server. Most of the code remains unchanged, but I will provide all the functions here to keep it clear.

```
function processSignalingMessage(message) {
    var msg = JSON.parse(message);
    if (msg.type === 'CHATMSG') {
        onChatMsgReceived(msg.value);
    } else if (msg.type === 'offer') {
        pc.setRemoteDescription(new
RTCSessionDescription(msg));
        doAnswer();
    } else if (msg.type === 'answer') {
        pc.setRemoteDescription(new
RTCSessionDescription(msg));
    } else if (msg.type === 'candidate') {
        var candidate = new RTCIceCandidate({sdpMLineIndex:m
sg.label, candidate:msg.candidate});
        pc.addIceCandidate(candidate);
```

5. The following piece of code contains the necessary improvements. In the original code, the client used to receive the GETROOM message only when creating a new virtual room. After we make changes in our signaling server, the client will receive this message in both cases: when they create a new virtual room and when they join an existing virtual room.

```
    } else if (msg.type === 'GETROOM') {
```

6. In both cases, the client will also get TURN credentials from the signaling server. These credentials should then be used by the client when authenticating on the TURN server.

7. We have to check whether we (the client) want to create a new room or join the existing room. In the first case, we need to store the received virtual room number by using the following code:

```
        if (!initiator) {
```

```
        room = msg.value;
        OnRoomReceived(room);

    }
```

8. The following function is absent in the original code of *Chapter 1, Developing a WebRTC Application* and is introduced in this chapter. This function will parse the message received from the signaling server, extract TURN credentials from it, and then store them in a variable.

```
        initICE(msg);
```

9. After we parse TURN credentials from the signaling server, we are ready to establish a peer connection. Thus, we call dogetUserMedia here, and it will call the appropriate "create peer connection" function.

```
        doGetUserMedia();
    } else if (msg.type === 'WRONGROOM') {
        window.location.href = "/";
    }
};
```

10. The following function is introduced in this chapter. It will parse a message received from the signaling server and extract the TURN credentials to be used further.

```
    function initICE(m) {
        var iceServers = [
            {
                'url' : m.url,
                'credential' : m.credential,
                'username' : m.username
            }
        ];
```

11. The following pc_config variable is used in the createPeerConnection function. In the original code, this variable was statically defined. Now, we assign an appropriate value to it dynamically according to the data received from the signaling server every time we want to establish a new peer-to-peer connection.

```
        pc_config = {"iceServers": iceServers};
    }
```

Thus, each time we will get new TURN credentials – temporary and time limited.

Starting the application and testing

Now it's time to start our application and test the TURN authentication. First, we need to start our TURN server that we built and configured in the previous sections of this chapter. In the command line, run the following command:

```
/usr/local/bin/turnserver
```

The preceding command will start the TURN server. If you set the verbose mode in the configuration file as described in an appropriate section in this chapter, you will see a lot of messages from the TURN server describing what is going on.

Next, start the signaling server. Use the following command:

```
erl -pa deps/*/ebin apps/*/ebin -sasl errlog_type error -s rtcserver_app
```

Next, open a new browser window and navigate to http://YOUR_DOMAIN:21000/.

Kindly note that you have to use the appropriate IP address or domain name where your signaling server is actually running.

If everything is OK, you will see a web form asking you to enter your e-mail address and password. As you know, we use static credentials for this authorization. So, please enter user@myserver.com in the e-mail field and secretword in the password field.

After you click on the **Submit** button, you should be redirected to the conference. html web page. Here you should see exactly the same UI that we developed in *Chapter 1, Developing a WebRTC Application*, that is, two video boxes and a chat area below. The browser will ask you for access to media and after approval, you will see an image from your webcam in the left video box.

In the chat area below, you should see a new URL with a virtual number at the end. Open this link in another browser or on another machine. If everything is going OK, peer connection will be established and both peers will see each other.

Now take a look at the terminal where you started the TURN server. If you have set the verbose parameter in its configuration file, you will see something very similar to the following information:

```
129: session 128000000000000001: new, username=<1395607096:<0.173.0>>,
lifetime=3600

129: session 128000000000000001: user <1395607096:<0.173.0>>: incoming
packet ALLOCATE processed, success

129: handle_udp_packet: New UDP endpoint: local addr 176.58.121.75:3478,
remote addr 89.209.127.164:50186

130: session 128000000000000007: user <>: incoming packet BINDING
processed, success
```

```
130: session 128000000000000009: user <>: incoming packet message
processed, error 401

131: session 128000000000000009: new, username=<1395607078:<0.170.0>>,
lifetime=600

131: session 128000000000000009: user <1395607078:<0.170.0>>: incoming
packet ALLOCATE processed, success

131: handle_udp_packet: New UDP endpoint: local addr 176.58.121.75:3478,
remote addr 89.209.127.164:52914

131: session 128000000000000010: user <>: incoming packet message
processed, error 401
```

You can see the TURN credentials there. Kindly note that "error 401" is a normal part of the TURN authentication process. If the TURN authentication fails, you will see something like "can't find user credentials" in the log.

Now, let's connect to the TURN server console and look deeply into what's going on. Open a new terminal and execute the following command:

```
telnet localhost 5766
```

By using this command, we connect to the running TURN server via the telnet protocol. By default, it will listen on `localhost` and TCP port `5766`. If you changed these parameters in the server's configuration, change them in the command appropriately.

After the command connects to the TURN server console successfully, you will see something similar to the following information:

```
Connected to localhost.
Escape character is '^]'.
TURN Server
rfc5766-turn-server
Citrix-3.2.2.910 'Marshal West'
Type '?' for help
```

Now we're in the TURN console. Here we can execute a limited set of special commands to control the server and get details on its state. For getting help, type ? and press *Enter*; this will print a list of the available commands with a brief explanation.

What we're interested in is the TURN sessions' statistics. Type the `ps` command in the console, and it will show a list of live TURN sessions with appropriate details as follows:

```
> ps
```

The result of the `ps` command is as follows:

```
7) id=128000000000000004, user <1395607096:<0.173.0>>:
   started 78 secs ago
   expiring in 3522 secs
   client protocol UDP, relay protocol UDP
   client addr x.x.x.x:58454, server addr y.y.y.y:3478
   relay addr x.x.x.x:63599
   fingerprints enforced: ON
   mobile: OFF
   SHA256: OFF
   SHA type: SHA1
   usage: rp=2, rb=172, sp=1, sb=120
    rate: r=0, s=0, total=0 (bytes per sec)


8) id=128000000000000010, user <1395607078:<0.170.0>>:
   started 76 secs ago
   expiring in 524 secs
   client protocol UDP, relay protocol UDP
   client addr x.x.x.x:52914, server addr y.y.y.y:3478
   relay addr x.x.x.x:50796
   fingerprints enforced: OFF
   mobile: OFF
   SHA256: OFF
   SHA type: SHA1
   usage: rp=2, rb=140, sp=1, sb=120
   rate: r=0, s=0, total=0 (bytes per sec)


Total sessions: 8
```

Here, you can see that we have two sessions. Actually, it says the total number of sessions is eight, and it is true. I just cut out the extra sessions because they're not relevant to the demo application.

If you see a session list similar to the preceding one, it means that the TURN authentication is working fine.

Summary

In this chapter, we learned more on security in the scope of developing WebRTC applications. We learned how to build and deploy TURN servers. We also learned in detail the TURN server's configuration options.

We modified the original code from *Chapter 1, Developing a WebRTC Application*, and integrated the application with our own TURN server.

In the next chapter, we will learn how to develop mobile applications that utilize the WebRTC API's features.

5
Mobile Platforms

In the previous chapter, we learned how to make our WebRTC applications secure. We covered HTTPS and SSL-secured WebSocket. We learned how to deploy and configure the TURN server, built our own TURN server, and integrated it with our developed WebRTC application. We introduced the TURN server's authentication mechanism as well.

In this chapter, we will talk about developing WebRTC applications for mobile platforms. We will also talk about mobile browsers and native applications. We will learn how to build the WebRTC native demo application for two mobile platforms. We will learn about the software developing kits that are available today and also learn which ones can help us develop in platforms where WebRTC is not natively supported yet.

Preparing the environment

In this chapter, we will compile a WebRTC demo application for Android and use a Linux box for this task. So, it is highly recommended that you prepare an x64 Linux box—you can use a virtual machine for this (for example, VMware or Oracle VirtualBox). It is also recommended that you use an Ubuntu distribution—the examples and code are not dependent on any particular distribution of Linux, but you will need to install additional packages and they may have different names for different distributions.

We will also build and compile a WebRTC demo application for iOS (as a native application). So, you will need a Mac OS X for this task. If you don't have a Mac computer, perhaps, Mac OS X running in a virtual machine (for example, VirtualBox or VMWare) could work here too, but I didn't test this nonofficial way, so there is no guarantee. Kindly note, you need to own a legal copy of Mac OS X license to run it legally under a virtual machine.

Supporting WebRTC on mobile platforms

Until now, we learned how to support WebRTC on desktops only. In the mobile world, it is not as good as it is on desktops. Mobile devices are something totally different and have their own way. Therefore, WebRTC is also something different in the mobile word.

For desktop applications, we considered using Google Chrome and Firefox, mostly. They both support WebRTC more than the other browsers. From *Chapter 1*, *Developing a WebRTC Application*, you know that Microsoft Internet Explorer and Safari don't support WebRTC yet. You also know that Opera is working on this standard and supports WebRTC partially.

In general, we can say that WebRTC is supported on desktop platforms—you need just a web browser and you need not care about the desktop's hardware and other software.

Unfortunately, the support of WebRTC on mobile platforms is as good as it is on desktops. Today (the beginning of 2014), there is no mobile device shipping with out-of-the-box WebRTC support in it. There is no public information on the known roadmaps for such support from any of the vendors in the world.

For a mobile device, it is not enough to just use a Chrome mobile because it will probably work for an Android device but won't work for iPhone.

In this chapter, we will talk about this issue and also discuss all the possible solutions that we could go with.

In the mobile world today, the following are the three possible consumption modes for WebRTC:

* The native browser
* The browser application
* The native application

Let's look at the current status of the WebRTC support for the most popular mobile platforms.

Android

In the past year, the Firefox community presented the Firefox web browser for Android with HTML5 and WebRTC support enabled out of the box. Now it is possible to make video calls on Android mobile devices using the WebRTC and Firefox mobile web browser.

These are the following three main WebRTC components that are supported in Firefox for Android:

- `getUserMedia`: This provides access to the user's webcam and microphone
- `PeerConnection`: This enables calls from one browser to another
- `DataChannels`: This establishes peer-to-peer data transfer between browsers

This is what authors say on this news at `https://blog.mozilla.org/blog/2013/09/17/webrtc-now-available-across-mobile-and-desktop-with-new-firefox-for-android-compatibility/`:

> *"WebRTC has been available in Firefox for Windows, Mac, and Linux since June, and today (September 2013) we add Android to our products that support WebRTC.*
>
> *We can't wait to see what cool new experiences leveraging WebRTC the developers will create!"*

Google Chrome for Android supports WebRTC as well. Here, the situation is very similar to the desktop world. The most interesting features usually first appear in Chrome, and after some time, they appear in Firefox.

So, for Android, you also have Chrome and Firefox. Other browsers don't support WebRTC yet. Nevertheless, the code base that Chrome and Firefox use is open source, and we can hope that the other browsers will introduce the support of WebRTC in the near future.

iOS

WebRTC is not supported on iOS for now. Apple did not implement any kind of support on Mac OS X or iOS, although WebRTC works well on Mac when using Chrome, Firefox, or any other browser that supports WebRTC. Nevertheless, none of these browsers support WebRTC on iOS (the mobile OS from Apple).

Today, your WebRTC applications won't work on Apple mobile devices, iPhone, iPad, and many others. They won't work out of the box, at least.

There is a web browser from Ericsson—Bowser. Most people have not even heard of this browser. Bowser is an experimental web browser for mobile devices, developed by Ericsson, and it supports WebRTC out of the box.

Bowser is available for Android and iOS. You can find its home page at `http://labs.ericsson.com/apps/bowser`.

It works on Android devices and iPhone/iPad. Bowser is available at Google Play and Apple App Store, so you can install it on your device in a native way. Please note that Android is supported for Version 4 and higher.

Today, the friendly way to support your WebRTC application on iOS is to ask your customers to use Bowser. Another way is to develop a special native application for Apple mobile devices. This is out of scope of this book, but we will touch on this topic later.

According to IT rumours, there is a big chance that Apple will introduce its support to WebRTC in iOS 8.

Windows Phones

Microsoft doesn't support WebRTC on desktop or mobile platforms. As you know from *Chapter 1, Developing a WebRTC Application*, Microsoft Internet Explorer doesn't support WebRTC, but on the desktop, you can just use another web browser.

For mobile devices, the situation is very similar to the Apple mobile platform — there is no support of WebRTC for Windows Phone yet. According to Microsoft's claims, they will introduce support of WebRTC after the standard is completed.

Today, your Windows Phone customers can't use your WebRTC applications. There is no known way to beat this situation.

The only reasonable way that remains is to develop a native application. Nevertheless, there are almost no doubts that Microsoft will take steps towards this path and introduce WebRTC support in the next versions of the Windows Phone platform.

Blackberry

WebRTC applications are not supported on Blackberry. For now, none of the web browsers in Blackberry support WebRTC in any way. It seems that there is no confirmed way to compile a native application that could utilize the WebRTC API.

Therefore, you should remember that your Blackberry customers should use any other mobile platform in order to use your WebRTC applications.

Nevertheless, this situation might change later on.

Utilizing WebRTC via a native browser

Utilizing WebRTC via the native browser means that the mobile device users can utilize the WebRTC features by just using the native web browser of the device. This is the most comfortable and convenient case for you and your customers. In this case, the device is always ready to work with WebRTC without any additional steps or configurations.

Today, this is the case with Android devices that are Version 4 or higher. As we discussed previously, you can use Chrome (the native web browser for Android) for mobile devices — both Chrome and Mozilla Firefox support WebRTC features not only on desktop systems, but also on the Android mobile platform.

Apple still doesn't show any activity regarding implementing support of WebRTC in their mobile devices. Today (in the middle of 2014) iOS 7 doesn't support WebRTC at all. So, your customers won't be able to use the native web browser, Safari, which uses your WebRTC applications, so your customers can't use the native browser, Safari, it just won't work with WebRTC.

Microsoft did not introduce WebRTC in Windows Phone 8, but they will probably do that later when they introduce it for Internet Explorer.

Utilizing WebRTC using browser applications

Utilizing WebRTC using browser applications means that a third-party application (a non-native web browser) can be used on a device in order to implement and utilize the WebRTC features. For now, we know of only one third-party application, and that is Bowser, as we have discussed this previously.

Bowser is developed by Ericsson and is available for two platforms — Android and iOS. The main problem with Bowser is that it seems like Ericsson hasn't invested much time in developing it. The last version at the time of writing this chapter is the one released in 2012, and it might be not be fully compatible with the last WebRTC API.

Another problem is that Bowser is not available in the US App Store for some reason. So, you will probably need to switch to another App Store account (non-US) in order to install Bowser.

Another third-party browser is Opera. I'm sure you've come across this great browser on the desktop and have probably used it earlier. As you probably know, Opera is available not only for desktop systems, but also for mobile platforms.

Opera has also implemented the WebRTC features (at least most of the main features), but it hasn't implemented WebRTC for mobile devices yet. Nevertheless, they did a great job on desktops and continue to do so. Thus, we can hope that Opera mobile will get the WebRTC support in the near future (there even is a chance that by the time you're reading these lines, the Opera mobile has actually started supporting WebRTC already).

The rest of the available mobile browsers (for example, Dolphin and the others) don't support WebRTC as of now.

So today, probably the most friendly and acceptable way to get iOS users from your WebRTC service is to ask them to use the third-party browser—Bowser (or Opera mobile in the future). The native support is supposed to appear in iOS 8. Another solution is to develop a native application.

Developing native mobile applications

As you can understand, WebRTC does not have wide support in mobile world yet (I'm writing these words at the beginning of 2014). So, the possible solution might be to develop a native application that utilizes the WebRTC API and integrates it into a service.

In general, this is not a good way to go. The main feature of WebRTC is a cross-platform solution. It requires no additional software, no plugin, and no installations. Just open your web browser, and there you go. However, the world is not perfect.

Anyway, for some cases, this way can be very appropriate because a native application can utilize some device-specific functionality and features that are not available in a web browser, or maybe these features are not supported by HTML5 browsers at all.

The WebRTC code is open source and is available for everyone. It is well documented and is supplied with examples and a demo application. In this chapter, we will also learn how to compile a native WebRTC application for Android and iOS. It is not a complete solution, of course, but it can be a good starting point.

Looking at WebRTC on mobile platforms

In the previous chapters, we learned how to develop WebRTC applications for the Web. We used the Google Chrome and Firefox web browser to test our applications. Also, we know that Opera supports the WebRTC API partially (the support is getting wider and better day to day). Now, what about mobile platforms?

WebRTC is open source and is used by Google, Firefox, and other big companies. Although mobile platforms have a variety of standards, API, software and hardware interfaces, there are many issues that need to be solved in order to make WebRTC friendly on mobile devices. Mobile platforms can be divided into two main categories — hardware and environment.

Hardware

Today, there are a lot of different mobile devices in the world. These devices have different hardware base that may require special handling:

- **Physical forms and display**: A lot of mobile devices have different form factors. This means that an image on one device will appear differently on another device due to another aspect ratio and resolution. What should happen if I use Version 5 of a Samsung phone and Version 10 of an HTC pad?

- **Audio**: Different devices have different configurations and realizations of the built-in audio system and attendant hardware. For example, there are a lot of Android-based devices with many differences between them that require special handling or a specific software API. Also, different mobile devices may use different kinds of audio/video codecs.

- **The photo/video camera resolution**: Different camera and screen resolutions lead to different qualities of image and video streaming quality.

- **The CPU architecture**: The mobile device should have at least the ARMv7 architecture of CPU and the NEON extension enabled in order to support the video features for WebRTC. Although audio features can be used without NEON, there may be a problem with using the native code libraries that should be compiled for the specific CPU architecture type.

- **The CPU power**: A device should have a powerful CPU to be able to process the video in real time. We don't need to just capture the video and display it on the screen. We need to encode it and transmit it over the network. So, definitely, the central processor unit can be a limiting factor in such kinds of work. The CPU power can be saved if the mobile device supports audio acceleration. Nevertheless, many devices don't support audio acceleration yet. Of course, a WebRTC application would work better by enabling this feature.

- **Sensors**: Most of the mobile devices can usually change the display orientation according to its physical orientation. This also affects the image generated by the device and the way it is displayed on the device's screen.

- **Battery**: If you have a rich media device, you probably know that audio/video consumes battery very intensively. For WebRTC applications, for which the video and audio is the key feature, this topic is very important.

Environment

Mobile devices usually work in different environments; they are often moved from one surrounding to the other. Of course, this produces new kinds of problems that are usually not presented on desktop systems and that need to be solved:

- **Changes in the connection state**: The mobile device usually automatically looks for the available networks such as the cellular network, WiFi, Bluetooth, or whatever it can find. The device can switch between networks automatically (and usually, switch from the GSM Internet to the Wi-Fi Internet, for example, in order to save money). There should be a strategy to handle such connectivity changes. If a device changes the connectivity, there has to be a way to keep the WebRTC session alive.

- **Profiles**: When a mobile device switches between networks, as discussed previously, it usually also switches between the network profiles. A user may change the position, and the network jitter or bandwidth can be changed as a result. If you are in a car cell, handoffs can occur or there could be glitches in the connectivity. A WebRTC mobile application (or a WebRTC mobile device implementation) needs to take into account elements such as the bandwidth, frame rate, and resolution adaptation, and behave in an appropriate way. With this in mind, you might be interested to read about **Mobile IP Interactive Connectivity Establishment (M-ICE or Mobile ICE)** at `https://tools.ietf.org/html/draft-tschofenig-mip6-ice`.

- **Light**: We're talking about mobile devices, so a mobile device can be moved from one place to another and as a result, we may get the light changed — it can be dimmer, for example. It will also affect the remote side, of course. Sure, the same is relevant for a usual desktop system. Nevertheless, mobile devices are more mobile and such kinds of problems are more relevant for them than for desktops.

- **Speaker, microphone, and noise**: Usually, mobile devices have very tiny speakers and microphone as compared to notebooks or desktop systems. However, they still have to provide the same good quality. In general, because of small dimensions, the audio components of mobile devices have to support good noise suppression, echo cancelation, and other mechanism and technologies to make the quality of sound acceptable.

- **Network**: We discussed NAT, the ICE framework, STUN and other cool words in *Chapter1, Developing a WebRTC Application*. You probably remember that WebRTC contains good mechanisms to work with firewalls and NAT. Nevertheless, you also probably remember that this is not so easy, and in many cases, it leads to annoying issues. Please note that this is even more hard and annoying in the world of mobile devices. NAT and firewalls are usually kind of a pain on mobile platforms. Also, many operators use proxy servers to provide Internet access to their customers, which can also produce additional complexity to the situation.

The bottom line is that there are many questions/issues in mobile platforms that need to be solved to get a good WebRTC implementation. Today, there is a lack of WebRTC support on mobile devices. Nevertheless, the WebRTC code base is growing every day and is becoming better and better, and probably in the near future, we will get it on mobile platforms that are as good as desktops. Meanwhile, we can use workarounds.

Using third-party libraries and SDKs

WebRTC is very popular and is definitely a hot topic. So, many companies started developing software development kits for it. Using such kinds of SDKs, you can simplify the development process. For example, some companies even provide some kind of cloud TURN servers. Some services can even route calls to **Public Switched Telephone Network (PSTN)**.

Also, most of these SDKs provide support to develop native applications. We will talk about a list of such companies and their SDKs. Actually, there might not be pure WebRTC APIs on the top layer of such SDKs. So, it is recommended that you do not tie your application with them too closely.

Some of the SDKs provide cross-platform tools. For example, Appcelerator and PhoneGap both offer the HTML5 wrapper along with native API layers to users. They can also provide the WebRTC support; then web developers would be able to do the same type of development for both mobile and desktop systems.

The following links are mostly to cloud services:

- `http://www.twilio.com`: This is for the cloud communication. It includes APIs for voice, VoIP, and SMS messaging

- `http://voxeo.com`: This is for the hosting and development of the IVR platforms

- `http://www.appcelerator.com/`

The following are the SDKs and additional services:

- `http://www.addlive.com/platform-overview/`
- `http://tokbox.com/opentok/libraries/client/`
- `http://www.frozenmountain.com/downloads#icelink`
- `http://phonegap.com/`

Building a WebRTC native demo application

As we just learned, many mobile devices don't support WebRTC out of the box. For some of these devices, we can use third-party web browsers, but for the rest, there is no good solution.

Nevertheless, one of the options to support WebRTC on such devices is to develop a native application that could utilize the WebRTC features that are being integrated into your service.

Developing mobile applications is a vast topic and is definitely out of scope of this book. Therefore, we will not delve deep into the native mobile application's development process, but we will learn how to get the WebRTC demo and build it for two platforms: Android and iOS.

So, in the following sections, we will learn how to get a demo application, build it, and test it. Although we will learn the basic cases only, we will not delve deep into specific fields of mobile development.

Firstly, we need an application for Android-based devices. We will build it using an Ubuntu x64 Linux box. Of course, you can use any other Linux distribution you like, but it should be x64 (this is the limitation of Android SDK).

After that, we will build a demo application for iOS. Here you will need Mac OS X. It is possible to use Linux box for this task as well. Nevertheless, I use MacBook Pro with Mac OS X installed on it and I'm not sure if using Linux for this task could be successful.

Building a WebRTC demo application for Android

Until now, we learned how to develop web-based WebRTC applications and services. Your customers can use them just via a web browser. Android has good support for WebRTC in the native mobile browser (and is the Google Chrome mobile) as far as third-party web browsers like Firefox are concerned.

Nevertheless, in some cases, you might want to develop a native Android application that could utilize the WebRTC features and closely integrate them with your service. For example, an in-browser application can't handle video/audio calls in the background. In other words, your customer will have to keep the web browser open in order to use your service and remain online. Although you may want to implement such kinds of features, for this situation, it is a good idea to consider developing a native mobile application that could utilize specific platform features like the possibility of being in the background and keep handling the WebRTC session, use push notifications, and so on.

In the following sections, we will learn how to get a demo application based on the Google Chromium code and how to build it. You can then take this demo application and use it as your basic code, improve it, and extend it in order to develop your own service-specific application.

Configuring the build environment

As we discussed previously, we need a Linux-based box. In particular, we will use Ubuntu Linux x64. No need to have a physical box, of course; we could use some virtualization products, such as Oracle VirtualBox or VMWare, or whatever you like best.

Please note that Linux should be x64. This is a limitation of Android SDK, and we won't be able to build the application on an x32 machine. The following steps will help you in preparing the build environment, we will install and configure the necessary software and libraries::

1. Firstly, we need to make some preparations and install development tools and libraries. Here, we're installing the code versioning tools, Git and subversion; they're used to get the source code from the Google repository. These tools can be installed by executing the following command:

   ```
   sudo apt-get install git git-svn subversion
   ```

2. Next, we need to download and prepare the Chromium depot tools.
    They're supported by Google and are required to compile the WebRTC code.
    To install them, open a new terminal and execute the following commands
    in the command line:

```
mkdir -p ~/dev/webrtc
```

```
cd ~/dev/webrtc
```

```
git clone https://chromium.googlesource.com/chromium/tools/depot_
tools.git
```

3. After the depot tools have been downloaded, we need to add them into the
    PATH variable by executing the following command:

```
export PATH=$PATH: `pwd`/depot_tools
```

 Please note that these changes will come alive during the current
terminal session only. They will be lost if you log in again. If you want
to save the new PATH environmental variable, you should add an
appropriate command into your .bashrc file. Here, I assume that you
will use the bash shell. If you use any other (for example, ZSH) shell,
use the appropriate resource file (.zshrc for ZSH).

It might be more comfortable for you to just open the shell resource file and edit it
manually. However, the main task is to add the full path to the depot tools in the
PATH variable.

After this operation, log in to the Linux box again (log out and then log in). From the
command line, run the following command:

```
gclient
```

This command is from the depot_tools package. If you see something like command
not found, it means that the previous step was not completed successfully and it
can't find the path to the package.

After this command is executed, you should see a list of available client commands.
This means that you installed the depot tools correctly, and we can continue.

Next, we again need to install additional development tools, compilers, and libraries.
Perhaps some of these are already installed in the box. However, if some of these are
missing, there is a big chance that you will face problems trying to compile the code.
So, in the terminal, execute the following command:

```
sudo apt-get install g++ pkg-config gtk+-2.0 libnss3-dev libudev-dev
libudev
```

Now we're ready to download the source code and get a bit closer to development.

Obtaining the source code

The WebRTC demo application that we're going to build is part of the WebRTC code developed by Google and is located in its repository. This code is a set of components and libraries that implement the WebRTC API. Thus, we need to download the WebRTC code from the repo, and then we will build the demo application by performing the following steps:

1. Use following commands in order to pull down the source code:

   ```
   cd ~/dev/webrtc
   ```

   ```
   gclient config http://webrtc.googlecode.com/svn/trunk
   ```

2. After all the commands are executed, you should see a new file, .gclient, in the ~/dev/webrtc folder. Here, we need to do some magic; we need to indicate that we want to build Android applications under Linux.

3. Edit the .gclient file using any text editor you like and append the following line to the end of the file:

   ```
   target_os = ['android', 'unix']
   ```

4. Or, you can do this just from the command line by executing the following command:

   ```
   echo "target_os = ['android', 'unix']" >> ~/dev/webrtc/.gclient
   ```

   This will instruct the gclient tool that we want to pull down the required third-party libraries and other tools as well to build source code for the Android platform.

5. After you have modified this file, go to the ~/dev/webrtc folder by executing the following command:

   ```
   cd ~/dev/webrtc
   ```

6. Finally, execute the following command:

   ```
   gclient sync --nohooks
   ```

   By executing this command, you will start a sync of the WebRTC stuff source code. This will usually take some long time.

Installing Oracle JDK

To compile the WebRTC code, we'll need to install Oracle JDK. Usually, it is not installed on Linux boxes by default, in particular, in Ubuntu (there are license issues, you can read more details at `https://wiki.ubuntu.com/JavaTeam`). Although most of the code is native and uses the Android NDK, this is necessary to build the JAR and APK files at the end of the build.

We can install Oracle JDK by performing the following steps:

1. First of all, let's download the Oracle JDK installation distributive from its home page at `http://www.oracle.com/technetwork/java/javase/downloads/index.html`.

   Please note that we need the latest JDK Version 1.6. JDK 7 (as the just-released JDK 8) will not work and you will get errors trying to compile the code. At the time of writing this, the latest available version of JDK 1.6 is Java SE Development Kit 6u45.

   Also, please note that we need to download the x64 version of JDK. Java 6 is outdated already and might not be available on the main Oracle download page. If so, you should go to the Oracle Java Archive page and find JDK 1.6 there at `http://www.oracle.com/technetwork/java/javasebusiness/downloads/java-archive-downloads-javase6-419409.html`.

2. Assuming that the downloaded `.bin` file is located in your home (~) directory, we need to execute the following commands to install JDK:

   ```
   sudo mkdir -p /usr/lib/jvm
   ```

   ```
   cd /usr/lib/jvm && sudo /bin/sh ~/jdk-6u45-linux-x64.bin --noregister
   ```

3. The following set of commands will extract JDK from its installation package into the `/usr/lib/jvm` directory. After this is complete and the JDK is unpacked, we need to set the default values to use the newly installed Oracle JVM as opposed to OpenJDK VM, which is usually installed and used on Linux boxes (in particular, for Ubuntu) by default:

   ```
   sudo update-alternatives --install /usr/bin/javac javac /usr/lib/jvm/jdk1.6.0_45/bin/javac 50000
   ```

   ```
   sudo update-alternatives --install /usr/bin/java java /usr/lib/jvm/jdk1.6.0_45/bin/java 50000
   ```

   ```
   sudo update-alternatives --config javac
   ```

   ```
   sudo update-alternatives --config java
   ```

4. Next, we need to create a symbolic link in order to fix a small bug in the source code building's infrastructure scripts, as follows:

```
cd /usr/lib
```

```
sudo ln -s /usr/lib/jvm/jdk1.6.0_45 java-6-sun
```

5. Now, we need to set the JAVA_HOME environment variable by using the following command:

```
export JAVA_HOME=/usr/lib/jvm/jdk1.6.0_45/
```

6. Finally, let's check the Java version we're using, as follows:

```
java -version
```

If you see something like Java HotSpot build 1.6.0_45 and not something like OpenJDK, it means that the correct version of Java is installed and we can continue.

Preparing for compilation

In order to prepare for the compilation, we need to install some additional developer tools. In particular, we need to install Apache Ant (the Java build tool) and x32 bit compatibility libraries.

Please note that for different versions of Ubuntu and different Linux distributives, these libraries may have different installation package names, *ia32-libs-multiarch* or just *ia32-libs*. In the following simple steps, we will install necessary software that might be absent on your system:

1. To install the libraries, execute the following command:

```
sudo apt-get install ia32-libs-multiarch ant
```

2. Now it's time to complete the preparations. Execute the following commands in the terminal:

```
cd ~/dev/webrtc/trunk
```

```
source ./build/android/envsetup.sh
```

The command that is being executed will set up and configure the necessary Android dependencies.

Please note the leading period on the envsetup.sh script; this is really important as we need the variables to be set for the rest of the current terminal session.

3. Assuming that these commands ran without any errors, run the following command:

    ```
    gclient runhooks
    ```

    By executing this command, we will generate the necessary ninja gyp compilation scenarios. Ninja is a build tool that is used to compile the WebRTC source code. It is something similar to making tools from autotools and is widely used in Unix-like systems.

4. After this is complete, run the following command:

    ```
    android_gyp
    ```

At this stage, you may get an error with a message such as `content.gyp could not be found` — this is not something critical and can be ignored for now.

Installing Android Development Tools

Android Development Tools (ADT) are a set of developer tools for the Android platform. We will use ADT to deploy the demo application to an Android device and an Android emulator. By default, ADT is not installed on Linux (actually, it is not installed on Windows either), so we need to perform the following steps in order to install these tools:

1. Download the ZIP archive with the ADT package relevant for your OS on the home page at `http://developer.android.com/sdk/index.html#download`.

2. Unpack the archive into some folder (for example, `~/dev`) by running the following command:

    ```
    cd ~/dev && unzip ~/adt-bundle-linux-x86_64-20140321.zip
    ```

3. Set up the `ANDROID_HOME` environment variable as follows:

    ```
    export ANDROID_HOME=~/dev/adt-bundle-linux-x86_64-20140321/sdk
    ```

4. Finally, we need to update the Android demo project by running the following command to prepare it for compilation:

```
$ANDROID_HOME/tools/android update project -p ~/dev/webrtc/trunk/
talk/examples/android
```

Now we have Android Development Tools installed and can continue compiling the demo application.

Compiling the code

Congratulations! We are done with all necessary preparations at this stage, and now we are ready to get into the compilation process.

To start the source code compilation, execute the following command:

```
ninja -C out/Debug -j 5 AppRTCDemo
```

By executing this command, we're asking the ninja build tool to generate a debug version of the application using a maximum of five concurrent build threads.

Please note that you might face the following errors:

- {standard input}: Assembler messages:
- {standard input}:7095: Warning: end of file in string; '"' inserted
- g++: Internal error: Killed (program cc1plus)

Usually, this means that your machine has insufficient free memory (RAM) to compile the code. If you're running this under a virtual machine, try to add some more memory resources to it and restart the process.

The compilation process will take several minutes. This, of course, depends on your machine and available resources.

Finally, the building process is finished. Now let's take a look at the ~/dev/webrtc/ trunk/out/Debug folder. If no errors happen after the previous command, you should see the AppRTCDemo-debug.apk file there.

Running the Android demo application on an emulator

If you don't have an Android device, you can try to use an emulator and run the demo application on a virtual Android device. This is done by performing the following steps:

1. Before we run the application on the emulator, we need to create an Android virtual device by executing the following command:

   ```
   cd $ANDROID_HOME/tools
   ./android avd &
   ```

   This will start a special tool from Android SDK to create and configure virtual Android devices that can be used then by an emulator.

   Click on the **New** button at the right-hand side of the window and create a new virtual device named emul.

    Please note that it is highly recommended that you check the **Use Host GPU** checkbox when creating a virtual device. Otherwise, there is a high chance that the multimedia features won't work in the emulator.

2. Now, we can start the emulator by asking it to use the just-created virtual Android device by running the following command:

   ```
   ./emulator -avd emul &
   ```

   Wait for a while until the emulator loads and you will see a typical Android desktop.

3. Now let's check whether our emulator works fine and the virtual device is alive by running the following command:

   ```
   cd $ANDROID_HOME/platform-tools
   ./adb devices
   ```

   This command will list all the available connected Android devices. If the created virtual device and emulator are running, you will see a message similar to the following one:

   ```
   List of devices attached
   emulator-5554 device
   ```

4. Everything seems to be fine and we can deploy our demo application to the virtual Android device and check how our application works when it is being run under the emulator:

```
./adb install ~/dev/webrtc/trunk/out/Debug/AppRTCDemo-debug.apk
```

You will see something similar to the following message:

```
835 KB/s (2238319 bytes in 2.616s)
  pkg: /data/local/tmp/AppRTCDemo-debug.apk
Success
```

5. Now we have an Android virtual device running under the emulator and a deployed WebRTC demo application. Go to the emulator's window and on the desktop, you should see an icon of our demo application named AppRTC. You can click on the icon to run the application.

Running the Android demo application on your device

If you have any Android device, you can also deploy the demo application into the device. Usually, it is much easier to debug Android applications on hardware than on an emulator:

1. Connect your Android device to the machine via a USB (don't forget to enable the debug mode on the device). Please note that some additional drivers might be needed. When you connect the device, you can also use the command described in the third step of the previous section to list the connected devices.

2. If you see your device in the list of the connected devices, deploy the demo application to the device. Run the following command in the terminal:

```
cd $ANDROID_HOME/platform-tools

./adb -d install ~/dev/webrtc/trunk/out/Debug/AppRTCDemo-debug.apk
```

3. Now you should see the demo application on your physical device and be able to launch it. So, we can go to the next section and check how the application works.

Testing the Android demo application

Now, when you have the demo application deployed on a virtual device that is running under the Android emulator or on a physical Android device, you can launch it and check how it works.

Open a new web browser window on your desktop machine and navigate to `http://apprtc.appspot.com`.

This is a web resource maintained by Google Corporation itself and is used as a host web platform to test WebRTC applications and services. The main feature in this chapter is mobile clients—so it doesn't make sense to develop our own WebRTC service. We can use Google's resource for our tests.

Provide the browser access to your media (the camera and microphone) and write down the room number of the conference window.

Now launch the AppRTC application on your Android device and enter the room number as part of the URL. If everything goes fine, you will see that a direct peer connection is established between the Android device and the desktop machine, and you can see that the audio and video is exchanged between them.

If you have any issues, you can check the ADB log for any messages, errors, or exceptions. The log is produced by the AppRTC application.

Also, another useful Android SDK tool that can help you with debugging is logcat. You can find more details on their web page at `http://developer.android.com/tools/help/logcat.html`.

For details on how to work with ADB and other Android developer tools, please refer to the official Google documentation at `http://developer.android.com/tools/help/adb.html`.

Building a WebRTC demo for iOS

The following material is based on original article, which is available at `http://ninjanetic.com`.

As we learned earlier, there is no official support of WebRTC in iOS. The native web browser, Safari, doesn't support it at all. Third-party browsers such as Chrome and Firefox have limited support as of now.

Nevertheless, WebRTC for iOS is under active development. If you want to integrate this technology into an iOS application, you need to directly use the WebRTC libraries that implement the features. Fortunately, an Objective-C implementation exists as a part of Google WebRTC source code and is free to use. A demo application is also supplied with the Google source code pack.

In this chapter, we will try to use the WebRTC code and libraries from Google to build and test a demo application supplied with the code pack.

As I said, Apple doesn't invest in public WebRTC code, and therefore, the code that we will try to use is very raw. Therefore, integrating existing WebRTC libraries and code pieces into your project is not easy, and someone could even say that it is a total nightmare. The libraries and demo projects are set up to support a large number of platforms simultaneously, so the build system is extremely complicated and tricky. You can't just open a project in Xcode and use interface builders. If you want to integrate WebRTC into your iOS application, you have to deal with the command line a lot. This is not easy and is unfriendly, but the situation is getting better.

Why can't we just take the compiled ready-to-go libraries, link them to our project, and build on top of them? This is because WebRTC is still in the active development stage in general, and is very raw in the aspect of iOS; there is no official support from Apple.

The demo project supplied with the Google source pack only supports audio calls. Yes, that means no video out of the box. This is not because WebRTC doesn't support video on iOS yet. Almost all features have been implemented in Objective-C already. Nevertheless, to develop a native iOS application by using WebRTC is not easy work.

While developing a WebRTC native iOS application, you have to work directly with WebRTC libraries and source code. You will also need to actively use console commands and shell scripts building and compiling your project. Unfortunately, so far there isn't any ready-to-use solution to do such kind of work in Xcode. It may take a surprisingly amount of effort to build the demo project for the simulator, and then trying to get it to build for a device can be even more work. Nevertheless, in the following sections you will find the steps that could help you with this work.

Many people from the community try to step forward in this way. Also, you can find other projects that are related to supporting WebRTC on iOS. For example, this one: `https://github.com/gandg/webrtc-ios`.

In other words, there is no solution yet that could be used out of the box. In this chapter, we will try to build a demo application supplied with the Google WebRTC source code pack and test it with the `appspot.com` web resource maintained by Google, as we did in the previous section on an Android demo application.

Preparing the environment

To prepare the environment, you need to have a Mac OS X. Perhaps this can be done using a Mac OS X running in a virtual machine, but I didn't check. I used a MacBook Pro that runs OS X Mountain Lion.

You need Git and Subversion to be installed. By default, these tools are not supplied with Mac OS, so you will need to install them in some other way. I'd suggest that you use HomeBrew, `http://brew.sh`, or you can use any other package manager for Mac you like the best.

We also need Xcode Version 5.0 or higher with the command-line tools installed. You can install these tools in Xcode using this menu path by navigating to **Preferences | Downloads | Command Line Tools.**

If you're using an actual iOS device, you will need a valid development code signing identity and a properly provisioned iOS device attached to your computer. We will not cover this topic in detail here because it is very specific and is not a short subject. If you're a beginner in iOS development and need any help, please refer to the appropriate manuals to learn how to create a digital sign for iOS applications. For example, you can use this very detailed and well-explained manual at `http://www.raywenderlich.com/2915/ios-code-signing-under-the-hood`.

Creating a work directory

For our experiments, we need around 2 GB of free disk space. Create a new folder somewhere on your disk by using the following command:

```
cd -p ~/dev/webrtc
```

Downloading the source code

First of all, we need to download the source code pack. We did this in the previous section where we built a demo application for Android devices. Here, we can use the same code base, and if you completed the task of downloading the source code for Android, you don't need to repeat it and download the code again.

Many of the steps will be very similar (and some of them might even be identical) to the steps we performed to build an Android demo application in the previous section. In this section, we will touch on such steps briefly and refer to the previous section. Other details relevant to iOS will be explained in more detail.

Getting the chromium depot tools

If you have read the previous section, you probably have `depot_tools` downloaded from Google already. If so, no need to repeat this step. If not, grab the chromium `depot_tools` repository from `git` by using the following command:

```
git clone https://chromium.googlesource.com/chromium/tools/depot_tools.git
```

These are a bunch of tools used during the build process and they need to be in your path, so you will need to modify your `.bash_profile` file (or any other shell file) and modify the `PATH` line as follows:

```
export PATH=~/dev/webrtc/depot_tools:$PATH
```

Next, you will need to restart your terminal or rerun your bash profile so that the changes take effect. This can be done by using the following command:

```
source ~/.bash_profile
```

Downloading the WebRTC source code

Go back to your working directory and use the following commands to download the massive source repository:

```
cd ~/dev/webrtc
gclient config http://webrtc.googlecode.com/svn/trunk
echo "target_os = ['mac']" >> .gclient
gclient sync
sed -i "" '$d' .gclient
echo "target_os = ['ios', 'mac']" >> .gclient
gclient sync
```

This magic is very similar to what we used in the previous sections when building a demo application for Android. This will take a pretty long time so here we can take a break and have a hot beverage.

Building and running a demo application on the iOS 7 simulator

This source code is capable of building a number of different platforms and is configured for it by default. As we are only interested in building for iOS, we are going to create our own build script that is compiled and run exclusively for the iOS simulator.

Yes, we won't use Xcode, and we're going to build everything from the command line, by performing the following steps:

1. Firstly, we need to define some additional environment variables to prepare for the building process. Here, we also select `ninja` as the build system (we also did this for Android), as shown in the following code:

```
export GYP_DEFINES="build_with_libjingle=1 build_with_chromium=0
libjingle_objc=1"
export GYP_GENERATORS="ninja"
export GYP_DEFINES="$GYP_DEFINES OS=ios target_arch=ia32"
export GYP_GENERATOR_FLAGS="$GYP_GENERATOR_FLAGS output_dir=out_
sim"
export GYP_CROSSCOMPILE=1
```

2. Now, we start the building process using the following commands:

```
gclient runhooks

ninja -C out_sim/Debug iossim AppRTCDemo
```

3. Now we can launch the demo application in the iOS emulator by using the following command:

```
~/dev/webrtc/trunk/out_sim/Debug/iossim out_sim/Debug/AppRTCDemo.
app
```

If everything goes well, you will see your iOS simulator pop up automatically, and the test application will be launched. If you see any errors, check whether you did everything correctly and whether you have all the necessary components (described in this section) installed and working properly.

Now, to give it a try, you need to create a video session that the test application can connect to. For the Android application in the previous section, we will use the Google WebRTC platform, `appspot.com`, to test our demo application. The easiest way to do this is to perform the following steps:

1. Open a new web browser window on your computer or an Android device.

2. Navigate to `http://apprtc.appspot.com`.

3. Give the browser the right permissions to access your microphone and camera and wait for the video to show up.

4. Please note that the URL in your web browser has changed. It will now look something like this: `http://apprtc.appspot.com?r=xxxxxxxx`.

5. The number appended to the end of the URL is the room number — we used a very similar mechanism to develop our own WebRTC services in previous chapters. So, write down the number. Switch back to the iOS simulator and paste that number into the textbox. Press the **Join** button on the keyboard and it will go away.

6. So, if everything has been done correctly, you will see the demo application working on the iOS simulator. Please note that the simulator is not as powerful as an actual device, so it can take some time to establish a connection, and you may have to wait for a while until the magic begins.

Thus, we made it work on a simulator, and now it's time to do the same on an actual device.

Building and running a demo application on the iOS device

We need a slightly different set of actions to build and run the test application on a real iOS device. These actions are as follows:

1. First of all, we need to set up a set of environment variables. This is very similar to what we did in the previous section when compiling a demo application for the iOS emulator. Nevertheless, there are some minor differences. For example, we need to choose the arm7 architecture, as shown in the following code.

```
export GYP_DEFINES="build_with_libjingle=1 build_with_chromium=0
libjingle_objc=1"
export GYP_GENERATORS="ninja"
export GYP_DEFINES="$GYP_DEFINES OS=ios target_arch=armv7"
export GYP_GENERATOR_FLAGS="$GYP_GENERATOR_FLAGS output_dir=out_
ios"
export GYP_CROSSCOMPILE=1
```

2. After that, we can compile the project by using the following code:

```
gclient runhooks
ninja -C out_ios/Debug-iphoneos AppRTCDemo
```

3. To get our final step to work, we need to install an additional tool called `ideviceinstaller`. It's super easy to install using homebrew (although it takes a while to build):

    ```
    brew install ideviceinstaller --HEAD
    ```

    Homebrew is a great package manager for Mac OS x. If you don't have homebrew yet, please refer to their home page for details at `http://brew.sh`.

4. Now, it's time to do the magic. Attach your iOS device to the machine via the USB. Run the following command to deploy the application:

    ```
    ideviceinstaller -i trunk/out_ios/Debug-iphoneos/AppRTCDemo.app
    ```

If everything goes well, the upload will succeed and you'll notice a new demo application icon show up on your physical device. The preceding command will not automatically launch the application on the device (as it did it in case of the simulator), so just click on the icon to run the demo. To test the demo, just follow exactly the same set of steps that we performed to test the demo when using the simulator.

Fixing possible issues in iOS 7

The originally built scripts supplied with the WebRTC source code pack were designed with iOS 6 in mind, and they include an obsolete framework that is not available in iOS 7 SDK. Building the code for an actual iOS device might throw out an error that is similar to `ld: framework not found IOKit`. Fortunately, fixing this problem is as easy as deleting a few lines. Open `trunk/talk/libjingle.gyp` and search for `framework IOKit`.

There should be two instances of `framework IOKit` in the file. Just delete both of these lines.

Changing the code

If you want to develop your own iOS application by enabling the WebRTC features, you just need to use part of the Google WebRTC source pack. The following are the two key locations to start with:

*   `~/dev/webrtc/trunk/talk/examples/ios`: This is the demo application with high-level communication logic and UI. You can take this as the base for your own application.
*   `~/dev/webrtc/trunk/talk/app/webrtc/objc`: These are the Objective-C wrapper classes for the core communication libraries.

As long as you modify the code that is in place, the build scripts will automatically tie everything together and compile the finished demo application.

Summary

In this chapter, we learned about the issues that might occur when supporting and developing WebRTC applications for mobile devices. We discussed the possible limitations and traits of supporting and developing the WebRTC API on mobile platforms. We learned what we need to do with this in order to solve our tasks when the WebRTC features have not been fully implemented on some mobile platforms. We briefly discussed the existing third-party SDKs and frameworks to develop mobile applications that could be useful. In this chapter, we also learned how to build native WebRTC applications for Android and iOS devices. We also deployed and launched demo applications on real mobile devices as well as on virtual devices that run under a software emulator.

So, it seems that it is time for the final words.

Using this practice guide, we learned how to develop different kinds of rich media applications and services utilizing the WebRTC API. We have written most of the code and developed nice demo applications. We learned some concepts of other interesting technologies such as WebSockets and some features of HTML5. While developing our applications, we were also introduced to Erlang, and we built web applications using this language.

I want to thank you for all the time you've spent with me working on this book. I hope this little trip was really useful for you.

Index

U

Thank you for buying
WebRTC Blueprints

About Packt Publishing

Packt, pronounced 'packed', published its first book "*Mastering phpMyAdmin for Effective MySQL Management*" in April 2004 and subsequently continued to specialize in publishing highly focused books on specific technologies and solutions.

Our books and publications share the experiences of your fellow IT professionals in adapting and customizing today's systems, applications, and frameworks. Our solution based books give you the knowledge and power to customize the software and technologies you're using to get the job done. Packt books are more specific and less general than the IT books you have seen in the past. Our unique business model allows us to bring you more focused information, giving you more of what you need to know, and less of what you don't.

Packt is a modern, yet unique publishing company, which focuses on producing quality, cutting-edge books for communities of developers, administrators, and newbies alike. For more information, please visit our website: www.packtpub.com.

About Packt Open Source

In 2010, Packt launched two new brands, Packt Open Source and Packt Enterprise, in order to continue its focus on specialization. This book is part of the Packt Open Source brand, home to books published on software built around Open Source licences, and offering information to anybody from advanced developers to budding web designers. The Open Source brand also runs Packt's Open Source Royalty Scheme, by which Packt gives a royalty to each Open Source project about whose software a book is sold.

Writing for Packt

We welcome all inquiries from people who are interested in authoring. Book proposals should be sent to author@packtpub.com. If your book idea is still at an early stage and you would like to discuss it first before writing a formal book proposal, contact us; one of our commissioning editors will get in touch with you.

We're not just looking for published authors; if you have strong technical skills but no writing experience, our experienced editors can help you develop a writing career, or simply get some additional reward for your expertise.

Getting Started with WebRTC

ISBN: 978-1-78216-630-6   Paperback: 114 pages

Explore WebRTC for real-time peer-to-peer communication

1. Set up video calls easily with a low bandwidth audio only option using WebRTC.

2. Extend your application using real-time text-based chat, and collaborate easily by adding real-time drag-and-drop file sharing.

3. Create your own fully working WebRTC application in minutes.

Elgg Social Networking

ISBN: 978-1-84719-280-6   Paperback: 196 pages

Create and manage your own social network site using this free open-source tool

1. Create your own customized community site.

2. Manage users, invite friends, and start groups and blogs.

3. Host content: photos, videos, MP3s, podcasts.

4. Manage your Elgg site, protect it from spam.

5. Written on Elgg Version 0.9.

Please check **www.PacktPub.com** for information on our titles

HTML5 Game Development with ImpactJS

ISBN: 978-1-84969-456-8   Paperback: 304 pages

A step-by-step guide to developing your own 2D games

1. A practical hands-on approach to teach you how to build your own game from scratch.

2. Learn to incorporate game physics.

3. How to monetize and deploy to the web and mobile platforms.

WordPress and Flash 10x Cookbook

ISBN: 978-1-84719-882-2   Paperback: 268 pages

Over 50 simple and incredibly effective recipes to take control of dynamic Flash content in Wordpress

1. Learn how to make your WordPress blog or website stand out with Flash.

2. Embed, encode, and distribute your video content in your WordPress site or blog.

3. Build your own .swf files using various plugins.

4. Develop your own Flash audio player using audio and podcasting plugins.

Please check **www.PacktPub.com** for information on our titles

www.ingramcontent.com/pod-product-compliance
Lightning Source LLC
LaVergne TN
LVHW081343050326
832903LV00024B/1290